The Complete
Bankruptcy
Guide

for Consumers and Small Businesses:

Everything You Need to Know
Explained So You Can Understand It

By Sandy Baker

THE COMPLETE BANKRUPTCY GUIDE FOR CONSUMERS AND SMALL
BUSINESSES: EVERYTHING YOU NEED TO KNOW EXPLAINED SO
YOU CAN UNDERSTAND IT

Copyright © 2011 Atlantic Publishing Group, Inc.
1405 SW 6th Avenue • Ocala, Florida 34471 • Phone 800-814-1132 • Fax 352-622-1875
Web site: www.atlantic-pub.com • E-mail: sales@atlantic-pub.com
SAN Number: 268-1250

Library of Congress Cataloging-in-Publication Data

Baker, Sandy Ann, 1976-
The complete bankruptcy guide for consumers and small businesses : everything you need to
know explained so you can understand it / by Sandy Baker.
    p. cm.
Includes bibliographical references and index.
ISBN-13: 978-1-60138-310-5 (alk. paper)
ISBN-10: 1-60138-310-X (alk. paper)
1. Bankruptcy--United States. I. Title.
HG3766.B216 2010
332.7'50973--dc22
                              2010017421

Printed in the United States

PROJECT MANAGER: Shannon McCarthy • PEER REVIEWER: Marilee Griffin
EDITORIAL ASSISTANTS: Amber McDonald and Danielle Reed
INTERIOR DESIGN: Rhana Gittens
FRONT COVER DESIGN: Meg Buchner • megadesn@mchsi.com
BACK COVER DESIGN: Jackie Miller • millerjackiej@gmail.com

Printed on Recycled Paper

We recently lost our beloved pet "Bear," who was not only our best and dearest friend but also the "Vice President of Sunshine" here at Atlantic Publishing. He did not receive a salary but worked tirelessly 24 hours a day to please his parents. Bear was a rescue dog that turned around and showered myself, my wife, Sherri, his grand-parents Jean, Bob, and Nancy, and every person and animal he met (maybe not rabbits) with friendship and love. He made a lot of people smile every day.

We wanted you to know that a portion of the profits of this book will be donated to The Humane Society of the United States. –*Douglas & Sherri Brown*

The human-animal bond is as old as human history. We cherish our animal companions for their unconditional affection and acceptance. We feel a thrill when we glimpse wild creatures in their natural habitat or in our own backyard.

Unfortunately, the human-animal bond has at times been weakened. Humans have exploited some animal species to the point of extinction.

The Humane Society of the United States makes a difference in the lives of animals here at home and worldwide. The HSUS is dedicated to creating a world where our relationship with animals is guided by compassion. We seek a truly humane society in which animals are respected for their intrinsic value, and where the human-animal bond is strong.

Want to help animals? We have plenty of suggestions. Adopt a pet from a local shelter, join The Humane Society and be a part of our work to help companion animals and wildlife. You will be funding our educational, legislative, investigative and outreach projects in the U.S. and across the globe.

Or perhaps you'd like to make a memorial donation in honor of a pet, friend or relative? You can through our Kindred Spirits program. And if you'd like to contribute in a more structured way, our Planned Giving Office has suggestions about estate planning, annuities, and even gifts of stock that avoid capital gains taxes.

Maybe you have land that you would like to preserve as a lasting habitat for wildlife. Our Wildlife Land Trust can help you. Perhaps the land you want to share is a backyard—that's enough. Our Urban Wildlife Sanctuary Program will show you how to create a habitat for your wild neighbors.

So you see, it's easy to help animals. And The HSUS is here to help.

THE HUMANE SOCIETY
OF THE UNITED STATES.

2100 L Street NW • Washington, DC 20037 • 202-452-1100
www.hsus.org

ACKNOWLEDGEMENTS

As with the writing of any nonfiction book, the research and planning are demanding, but through it all, my husband, Owen, and the rest of my family were there for me. For their encouragement, even under deadline pressure, I thank them. I dedicate this book to them.

Contents

CH 3: THE CONSUMER BANKRUPTCY DETAILS YOU NEED   59

CH 4: YOUR PROPERTY DURING BANKRUPTCY   79

CH 5: COMPLETING CONSUMER BANKRUPTCY   127

Foreword

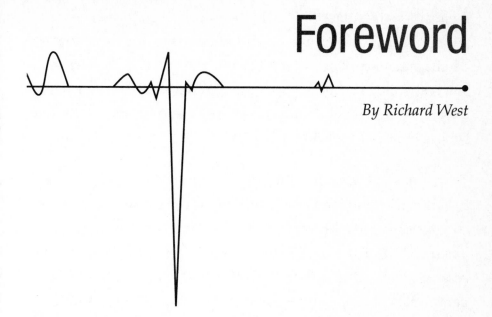

By Richard West

The current economy is forcing many consumers to look for options to deal with bills when they simply cannot pay them all. Job loss, medical emergencies, divorce, and other life-altering situations frequently result in lower income. This makes covering all of their living expenses and monthly obligations impossible. The bankruptcy system has always been the safety net for financial situations not capable of being resolved with less serious methods.

Consumers face a bewildering array of financial options, many contradictory in their claims. These options tend to be complicated and confusing. Declaring for bankruptcy, in particular, receives an enormous number of conflicting reviews and a tremendous amount of misinformation from a variety of sources.

When I started practicing bankruptcy law in 1986, there was very little consumer information available. Most people only knew what their friends, family members, and co-workers could tell them about the subject. Much of the information turned out to be wrong. Then, a surprising amount of attorneys did not know the details of bankruptcy, as it has been — and still is — an area of the law best suited for specialists. In fact, bankruptcy law was not on the bar exam when I became an attorney, and it is not a required subject in law schools today.

The Complete Bankruptcy Guide for Consumers and Small Businesses is an excellent source of information for consumers who are contemplating bankruptcy either for themselves or their small business, or for those who are currently going through the process and want to understand it better. Frequently misunderstood bankruptcy concepts are explained in plain, easy-to-understand language. The reader is taken through the process of each of the most common chapters of bankruptcy — 7, 11, and 13 — in a straightforward and comprehensible manner.

The many observations and recommendations about actions to avoid before filing a bankruptcy are particularly helpful. Bankruptcy rules are not the kind of common-sense notions that the average consumer would think them to be. This book helps the reader to avoid the pitfalls that are not obvious but could — and frequently do — have serious consequences in a bankruptcy case.

Bankruptcy attorneys, in my experience, generally do not have the time to explain in any significant detail the many steps that occur in a bankruptcy case. Consumers do not know what questions to ask, causing important details to be overlooked by both the attorney and the client. This book does a masterful job of identifying problem areas and explaining how difficulties with the court and bankruptcy trustee can be avoided.

Also helpful are the insights into life after bankruptcy, advice on matters involving credit before and after filing, and the excellent section on bankruptcy myths. Most people do not know much about bankruptcy or do not know how to apply their knowledge to their own filing. This book provides consumers a solid foundation of facts and explanations of bankruptcy concepts. After reading this book, consumers will have an accurate understanding of how bankruptcy really works.

Though not a substitute for legal counsel, the information in this book will assist anyone who is interested in learning about how the bankruptcy system works, what filing for bankruptcy entails, and what steps are involved when filing a bankruptcy case. Even if a consumer has chosen to be represented by an attorney, this book would be an excellent tool to understand the process and feel more comfortable with what is, for most, a very uncomfortable — even frightening — experience.

If a consumer does choose to file his or her own bankruptcy without counsel, *The Complete Bankruptcy Guide for Consumers and Small Business* is an excellent overview and fundamental analysis of bankruptcy law that delivers what it promises.

Richard West is the founder and managing partner in the law firm of West, Hurley, & Malkiewicz. He is a board-certified consumer bankruptcy specialist and limits his practice to consumer bankruptcy law, which he has been practicing since 1986. He attended St. Joseph's University for his undergraduate studies and law school at Temple Univer-

*sity in Philadelphia. He is a member of the National Association of Consumer Bankruptcy Attorneys, the American Bankruptcy Law Forum, the National Association of Chapter 13 Trustees, and the Ohio State Bar Association. His practice area includes the entire Southern District of Ohio. West has lectured frequently to attorneys on bankruptcy matters and has published numerous articles on bankruptcy law. He maintains a Web site at **www.debtfreeohio.com** with continuously updated consumer bankruptcy information and can be reached at **rew@ debtfreeohio.com**.*

Introduction

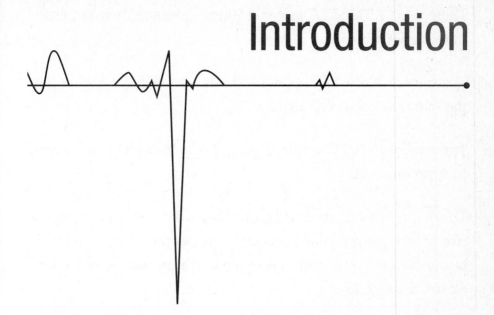

Bankruptcy is an ugly word — a word you never thought you would have to utter to family and friends when discussing your financial state. Yet, today more than ever, people need this resource to help them get back on track financially. Many people spend time considering whether bankruptcy is the right option for them, wondering and worrying if it is the best or only option. You are not alone. This book will help you decide if you should file and guide you through the process many Americans now find themselves struggling through.

The numbers are staggering. In the 12-month period ending December 31, 2009, there were 1,473,675 bankruptcy cases filed in the United States, according to the Administrative Office of the U.S. Courts. This was a 31.8 percent increase in this number compared to the previous year.

Take a closer look at the numbers. Of those filings, consider the following breakdown:

There were 1,050,832 Chapter 7 filings, up more than 41 percent from the year before.

There were 406,962 Chapter 13 filings, 11.9 percent higher than the same period a year before.

There were 15,189 Chapter 11 filings, up almost 50 percent from the previous year.

These numbers seem drastic, but they are likely to continue to rise in the coming years, especially as people struggle with the burden of debt under other economic strains, such as home foreclosure and job loss.

Many Americans need to use bankruptcy in order to get their lives back on track financially. Under U.S. bankruptcy laws, individuals have the right to file for bankruptcy in order to be free of the debt they cannot pay. This law is within the U.S. Code, and is formally U.S. Title 11-Bankruptcy. Is this the best resource for your financial problems? Bankruptcy is the right decision for many individuals struggling under financial burden and without recourse to dig out from that debt, and this book will serve as your guide through the process. When you file a petition for bankruptcy, you are requesting that your excessive debt be reorganized or discharged completely. Discharged debt no longer needs to be repaid. This legal process helps you manage debts you would not otherwise be able to repay in the long term.

However, there are consequences to filing for bankruptcy. You will face long-term difficulty using credit. You may pay more in interest rates on loans. Some insurance companies might charge you more. You will have difficultly building your credit score back up so that you can apply for and get new loans. It is possible to do so, but it is hard work. Considering these consequences, should you file for bankruptcy? In the end, only you can make this personal financial decision, so make it an educated decision. This book provides you with the foundation you need to make that decision. You will learn about bankruptcy for personal and business use. You will also learn how to recover from bankruptcy so that your financial future looks promising. The information in this book is designed to help you to make decisions about bankruptcy.

As you sit at your desk and look at a pile of bills, you might know you do not have the funds to pay. How could this happen to you? You thought you were making good decisions using credit cards or securing a loan. On the other hand, maybe you know what caused the debt to build, but you did not see any way to avoid this problem. Debt is oftentimes brought on by personal misfortune. Some of the most common reasons for filing for bankruptcy include job loss, medical bills, divorce, and small business failures. Small business bankruptcy happens because of poor financial management, poor economic circumstances, or a simple lack of planning. None of the individuals involved in these situations are specifically to blame for their acquired financial burden. However, it is the individual's responsibility to resolve these debts in some way. Bankruptcy is one option.

This book defines what bankruptcy is and provides you with the tools to understand your options. Do you need to wipe out your debt in total? Are you just looking for some way to reorganize it? Do you want to keep your business afloat? If so, there are options available to you. What is important here is that you take action now. Not only can financial burden hinder your ability to achieve financial goals, but it can also cause an incredible amount of stress from phone calls from creditors and worries about your future. Take the time to read this book first. Then, consult with a bankruptcy attorney. This book will explain how to find and use an attorney. If you do not plan to file over the next few months, ask your attorney to keep you up to date on changes, so that you can choose the best time to file.

Take all of these steps now so you can get relief sooner. You do not need to struggle financially. Many people can find new opportunities after bankruptcy. With the help of this guide, you will soon be on your way to doing just that.

CHAPTER 1

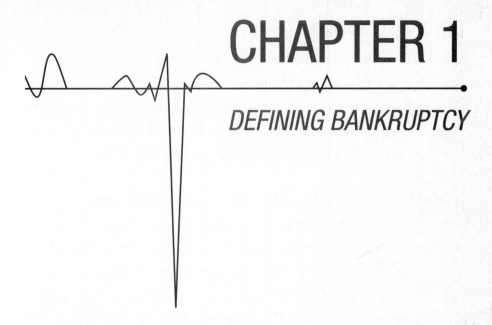

DEFINING BANKRUPTCY

Bankruptcy is not something you want to go through, but it may be something that you need to go through. It has consequences, but it can also allow individuals and small businesses a fresh start at rebuilding financial health. Before you decide if bankruptcy is for you, you should understand what it is and how it works.

The U.S. Constitution gives all Americans the right to file for bankruptcy, which simply means the forgiving of debts. When individuals, married couples, or businesses cannot repay their debts, a federal district court may allow the debts to be forgiven or reorganized to make them easier to pay. Under U.S. law, some types of property an individual owns may be liquidated and the profits paid to creditors. A **creditor** is someone who lends money, and a **debtor** is someone who borrows that money. Laws also protect some types of property from liquidation.

Defining Debt

What is debt anyway? Before going further, it is important to understand what this is and how bankruptcy affects it. Debt is any type of loan that you take out with the promise to the lender to repay. There are several types of debts, but they fall into two main categories: **secured debts** and **unsecured debts**.

As the name implies, secured debts are the type of debt that is secured by something. The most common forms of secured debt are mortgage loans and car loans, which are based on the value of the home and car. When you purchase a home, the mortgage you obtain is backed by the value of the home. Lenders, such as banks, will lend up to that value. If you stop paying your mortgage, the lender will foreclose on your home. The foreclosure process allows the lender to take back the home to repay the debt you owe. You lose the home, but the lender does not lose the principle lent to you to buy the home.

The other type of debt is unsecured debt, which is debt that is not backed by any asset. The most common form of unsecured debt is the credit card. When a lender issues a credit card, for example, the lender understands that there is no recourse for getting their money back should you default on the loan. This increased risk is why credit cards tend to have higher interest rates than home loans.

Why does this matter? As you will see in the following chapters, bankruptcy addresses debt by the type of debt it is. The secured debts may need to be repaid rather than completely wiped clean, which occurs with unsecured debts in some forms of bankruptcy. If the debt is not repaid, the lender can take back the asset.

Bankruptcy Basics

In 1978, the United States Congress enacted laws called the Bankruptcy Code. These laws have changed since that time, but they still hold the same purpose: They establish procedures of how bankruptcies are filed, including who can file them and how the process works. In 2005, new bankruptcy reforms went into effect, which made it harder for people to take advantage of the bankruptcy system. Prior to this time, lenders believed that consumers would specifically run up personal debt knowing they could file for bankruptcy without recourse. Today, it is harder to file for bankruptcy, as there are additional steps you will need to take.

The U.S. Constitution allows Americans and American businesses to file for bankruptcy. Article 1, Section 8 of the U.S. Constitution outlines the federal law that gives Congress the right to enact uniform law on bankruptcies. The Constitution states that Congress has the right "to establish an uniform Rule of Naturalization, and uniform laws on the subject of bankruptcies throughout the United States." This means that Congress has the right to establish a Bankruptcy Code that all states must follow.

The federal government mandates the Federal Rules of Bankruptcy Procedure, also known as Bankruptcy Rules, which includes mandating the procedures and the forms filed during bankruptcy. In 2005, Congress put in place a new set of laws to govern bankruptcies more closely. These laws tightened the way that bankruptcy could be used by consumers or small businesses. These laws, called the Bankruptcy Abuse Prevention and Consumer Protection Act of 2005, outline specific changes to the way that people could file for bankruptcy. These changes include:

- The establishment of a "means test" to determine if an individual will be able to repay some or all of his or her debt.

- An establishment of income levels to qualify for Chapter 7 bankruptcy.

- The addition of counseling requirements for some individuals.

- Higher accountability of lawyers and their actions; attorneys are unable to encourage you to file for bankruptcy just to make a profit.

- A rise in the costs of filing for bankruptcy.

- A new limit to the number of times bankruptcy could be filed for within a seven to ten year period for individuals and businesses.

The federal government also establishes bankruptcy courts; there is at least one bankruptcy court in each judicial district within the country. There are 90 bankruptcy districts across the United States. Each of these also has bankruptcy clerk's offices, which you will need to visit.

Within the courts, there are bankruptcy judges who decide on any matter that is necessary within the bankruptcy process. This includes making decisions on eligibility to file, as well as whether all debts will receive discharge. However, most of the actual work regarding your bankruptcy filing will happen outside of the courts through administrative means. A bankruptcy trustee, who is assigned to your business or individual case when you file, carries out this process. In most cases of bankruptcy, you will meet with a bankruptcy judge only for a few minutes toward the end of the process. In most cases, this judge is only looking for the reason for the bankruptcy and official word from you that you do want to file. Prior to this point, you may meet with the bankruptcy trustee, depending on the type of bankruptcy you are filing. In other cases, you will work strictly through an attorney.

There is a state implication in bankruptcy law, though. Although bankruptcies are governed specifically through the federal court system, each state has the right to make some specific modifications to these laws. These laws cannot and do not supersede any federal laws, but they can work alongside them. The most common element that differs from state to state is the exemptions, which allow some level of protection for your personal property. For example, in a total discharge of debt, any lender you have may wish to liquidate your assets so that the funds can be used to repay the loan. However, in order for this to happen, the amount of assets you have must be higher than the state's exemptions. Exemptions differ in type and amount by state, but they may include any of the following:

- **Homestead exemptions**: The amount of real or personal property you may have that is unavailable for creditors to liquidate. In some states, for example, your home may be exempt up to a specific dollar value in equity.

- **Insurance exemptions**: Most states limit the types and amounts of insurance protection you may have that are exempt from creditor liquidation.

- **Pension exemptions**: Most states do not allow pension payments to be used to repay creditors, because it is a form of retirement benefit.

- **Personal property**: Specific property types that are exempt from creditor liquidation generally include animals, household goods, clothing, appliances, and burial plots. Although not called a homestead exemption, these are similar; however, they are listed specifically on a state-by-state basis.

- **Public benefits**: Most states do not allow public benefits such as social security, veteran benefits, and workers' compensation, to be used to repay lenders.

- **Tools-of-the-trade exemptions**: If you need specific tools for your business, these may be exempt.

To find out what the exemptions are for your state, visit your state's bankruptcy court Web site or contact your attorney. For many people, meeting these limits is no problem. A common example of how a bankruptcy exemption can protect you has to do with your home. **Equity** is the value of your home subtracted by any mortgage loan or tax lien you may have against it. If you file for bankruptcy, you may be able to keep your home if the amount of equity you have is not higher than the state's homestead exemption. If your equity level is higher, you may need to sell the home to access the equity to repay your lenders.

Also note that there are federal exemptions. These are similar to those listed above, but in some states, the federal exemptions allow for you to keep a larger portion of your property. In some states, you can choose between taking the state or federal exemptions. *This is explained further in Chapter 4.*

Exemptions are there to protect individuals from being unable to support themselves after they file for bankruptcy, while still providing the lenders the right to take excess property to repay debts owed. Businesses do not have exemptions in most situations. Exemptions are generally a factor under Chapter 7 bankruptcy.

Bankruptcy chapters

Bankruptcy has several **chapters**, which simply refers to the place in bankruptcy code where the specific details are. The following explains a few of the differences in bankruptcy chapters.

Chapter 7 bankruptcy

For consumers, the most common form of bankruptcy is Chapter 7, because it releases individuals from debt. It is also known as liquidation. The process takes between four to six months to complete. You will need to file documents stating your need and reason to file. The courts must approve that request, taking into account the value of any assets and the need to repay creditors anything possible. At the end of that time, all debt included in the bankruptcy documents is forgiven. You may file Chapter 7 only once every six years. Bankruptcy filers lose any assets they have that are not exempt, but they no longer need to repay debts. *However, there are limitations on what is lost; turn to Chapter 4 for more information on these limitations.* Chapter 7 bankruptcy is best for those with few assets, little or no income, and those with excessive amounts of debt. Chapter 7 bankruptcy remains on your credit report for up to 10 years.

Chapter 11 bankruptcy

Chapter 11 bankruptcy is generally used by corporations or partnerships. This type of bankruptcy does not discharge debts, but instead, it allows the business to reorganize its debts to make them easier to repay. In most situations, the debtor will enter into a Chapter 11 bankruptcy plan with the goal of keeping the business alive and well while repaying creditors over a period of time. Those who are in business who file this form of bankruptcy want to keep their business going but are struggling to find a way to pay all of their debts immediately. The bankruptcy court oversees the repayment plan, which is designed to meet the business's needs specifically. *The second portion of this book explains the small business bankruptcy process.*

Chapter 12 bankruptcy

Chapter 12 bankruptcy is the least common form of bankruptcy. This part of bankruptcy code was written specifically for family farmers or family fishermen to aid them in times of hardship unique to their living situations. In short, anyone who has a regular annual income in this type of industry would use this type of bankruptcy. Under Chapter 12, some of the debt may be forgiven, but in most cases, a plan is worked out to allow the debtors to repay debts. Chapter 12 bankruptcy generally lasts between three and five years, during which the debtor repays the debt in installment payments. This particular plan is much like Chapter 11 or 13, but it is simplified to allow for the small-farming family to enter the process faster and with fewer limitations. A streamlined process is also less expensive than filing for Chapter 11 bankruptcy.

Chapter 13 bankruptcy

Chapter 13 bankruptcy is another option for those who are looking for a way to restructure their debt, also known as a debt adjustment. It allows individuals to temporarily stop financial legal action such as foreclosures and collections until the debt can be reorganized for the debtor with the court's help. The goal here is to create a plan that will allow the debtor to repay his or her debts over a period of three to five years. The bankruptcy court uses regular income information to determine how much of the debt you will repay as well as how much the payment is per month. This type of bankruptcy helps to extend secured date repayments over a longer time, such as your home loan. There are limitations on who can file for Chapter 13 — for example, incorporated businesses cannot — and it will also remain on one's credit report for up to seven years. You cannot file for Chapter 13 bankruptcy if you have filed for Chapter 7, 11, or 12 in the last four years, or if you have had another Chapter 13 bankruptcy filing in the previous two years.

Is Bankruptcy Right for You?

Now that you have had a quick look at what bankruptcy is, it is time to consider if bankruptcy is the right choice for your particular financial situation. Your primary goal should be to avoid bankruptcy if it is at all possible so you can avoid the consequences of not repaying your debt, such as a flawed credit report, which limits the amount of credit you can obtain in the future. You may also struggle with employers who will not hire individuals with a bankruptcy on file. First work through every other option available to you; then, if you still find bankruptcy is your only recourse, you should take advantage of this American right. The following information will help you make this important decision by quickly reviewing these options.

Methods to paying down debt

Besides making your monthly payments, what are the other methods you can try to dig out from debt quickly? There are several other options to consider before you actually file for bankruptcy, including working with lenders, credit-counseling services, and debt settlement program.

Working with lenders directly

One of the first things a consumer can do to get out of debt is to call each of his or her lenders directly and inform them of the problem, such as job loss or medical costs. Be completely honest and upfront and ask for aid in working out the debt with a lower payment. Do this as soon as you cannot make your payments. Most lenders will work with you because they know they will get far less if you do file for bankruptcy. Working with lenders directly may require the development of a payment plan, and most lenders will close the credit account, so you can no longer access it. They may be willing to lower interest rates or the amount of your monthly payment, depending on your need, but generally, you will keep paying interest so the lender keeps making money.

The key benefit of working with lenders in this manner is, you can keep your credit score in better shape in the short term when compared to filing for bankruptcy. Working with lenders also means you have to pay the debts you have incurred. If you have called the lender, and they are not able to help you in any way, that makes repaying the debt impossible; therefore, you may have to consider another option. Not all lenders are willing to be flexible, but it will not hurt to pick up the phone and call to discuss your options.

Consider credit-counseling services

A credit-counseling service is another option to consider. Under the new reforms of bankruptcy law, it is now a requirement for many individuals to work through a credit-counseling service before they will be able to file for bankruptcy. You can find credit counseling agencies in your local phone book. Call a nonprofit organization and learn about your options. There is usually a small fee to pay in using these organizations, but it is worth the minimal cost. You will complete a means test to determine if you must go through credit counseling. Those who may be able to repay some of what they owe will need to work through credit counseling. With this type of service, you will work with a counselor one-on-one. That counselor will work with you in several ways:

- He or she will help you create a budget that you will follow until you pay off your debt. The basis for the budget is your actual income. It takes into account all of your monthly payments as well as entertainment money, food money, and personal expenses, like getting a haircut.

- Credit counselors determine how much you can afford to pay each month to lenders. Then, they contact each of your lenders to work out a payment solution. The counselor might be able to get interest rates dropped. They also work with lenders to reduce the amount you owe as much as possible. The lender may agree to a lower monthly payment, too.

- After coming to an agreement with your lender, the counseling agency sets up a payment plan. You will make a monthly payment to the credit counseling agency, who will then farm out these funds to each of the lenders in the agreed upon amount. There is generally a low fee involved in the process, too.

- The goal of this plan is to pay off your debt in a short timeframe, usually less than three years.

Consumer credit-counseling services like these can affect your credit score negatively at first, because your creditors may report that you are not paying your debts as originally agreed. However, as you start to repay your debts, your credit score will improve. These services can often stop your creditors from taking legal action against you. At the end of the plan, you will need to work hard to reestablish your credit score and build your finances back up. This means making good financial decisions and using credit wisely. There is no limit to improving your credit score. Eventually, these accounts will fall off your credit report because delinquencies, such as late payments, are removed from credit reports after seven years. Over time, you can build your score higher than it was before. The process is not easy, but many find it a better option than filing for bankruptcy because this will stay on your credit report for up to ten years.

Debt settlement

Another solution for some individuals is debt settlement, which is the process of negotiating a deal with the lender in which you will pay less than your total debt owed in one payment. There are several key benefits to this, namely that you will pay far less in the long term for the debt. It also has less of a negative effect on your credit score than filing for bankruptcy because you are repaying your debt to some level. Still, this is not an easy option. In order to settle a debt, you will need to pay between 50 to 80 percent of the amount owed upfront. For instance, say your debt to a lender is $1,000, the lender may agree to a settlement of $750. However, they expect you to pay that $750 right away or over the course of a few weeks. If you do not have the funds necessary to pay a large chunk of money like this, repayment might not be right for you, or even possible. If you do have the funds available to make a settlement on the debts you owe, you can contact your lenders directly and negotiate with them.

Some businesses do offer specialized debt settlement services as third parties. They are not associated with the creditors directly. With these companies, you can contract with them to renegotiate your debt for you with the lenders. Their experience may be helpful in overcoming the debt, but it is important to factor in any costs associated with this type of debt plan. The cost of debt settlement is quite varied. Some companies charge a per transaction fee, while others charge a monthly fee for the service. This varies by establishment and location. Be sure to choose a debt settlement company with a good reputation, and be wary of any company that charges fees before performing any services.

If any of these methods of debt repayment are something you have yet to try, do so. You may find that repaying your debt is not as difficult as you thought it would be. Debt settlement, credit counseling, and working with lenders directly are all less destructive to your credit score and financial future than bankruptcy is.

Managing your debt

Perhaps you do not want to file for bankruptcy, but instead, you would like to find a way to manage your debt. If so, there are a few things to keep in mind before taking on this commitment. For some, the desire to repay debt is more than just ability. Many feel they are morally obligated to repay anything they owe. Even in this case, however, you have to consider how you will manage your debt.

To repay your debts, you need to focus on your **four walls** first. Those four walls are any type of bill that helps you to maintain your home and your job, including paying for food, shelter, transportation, and basic needs. This means you should first use your income to pay for your home mortgage and utilities because these are critical means for maintaining your health and well-being. After paying these, pay other secured debts, such as car loans. Because you may need the vehicle to get to your job, stay up to date on these payments. After paying off all remaining secured debts, repay your credit card debt or other unsecured debts you have, such as medical bills and personal loans. For many people, funds are depleted after paying their four walls, making it impossible to pay for unsecured debt. These individuals should consider bankruptcy.

Some people want to file for bankruptcy just to stop the phone from ringing off the hook. Creditors and collection agencies are annoying because they hope that you will do what it takes to silence them, which generally is making your payment. If you do not have the money to do so, though, you should know your rights according to The Fair Debt Collections Act.

- Creditors cannot call you at all times of the day and night. Generally, they are able to call between 8 a.m. and 9 p.m.

- Creditors cannot threaten you in any way. If they say they will call all of your friends or get you in trouble at work, report them to the Federal Trade Commission.

- Inform your creditors of your circumstances. Be sure they fully understand what your circumstances are, because most will work with you. Tell them when you are going to pay, and if you are considering bankruptcy, tell them this, too.

- If a creditor calls you at work, tell them you are unable to receive calls at your place of employment. They are required to stop calling work numbers at that point.

- Finally, if you do file for bankruptcy, you need only to provide the bankruptcy attorney's information one time to the lender. At this point, the creditors can no longer call you. They must refer all contact to your bankruptcy attorney.

Do not file for bankruptcy just to silence your creditors. However, if you do not have any resources to pay these lenders, realize that it will continue to get worse. Take steps toward bankruptcy to help stop the onslaught. If you keep avoiding lenders, they can sue you. You may even have **garnishments**, which are payments taken out of your paycheck that are paid directly to your lender, if you fail to take steps to resolve your debt. Garnishments are often the last step that a lender will take to collect a debt. The funds are taken directly from your check through your employer. You receive warning of pending garnishments through a court written letter. This often occurs if you have not responded to the lender or collection companies. Because you entered a legally binding agreement by agreeing to the terms of a credit card or loan, any lender has the right to sue you for repayment if you fail to meet those criteria. However, they are only likely to do this if they believe the expense of hiring an attorney is likely to produce a payment from you. For example, if you simply do not answer the phone when your lender calls month after month on a large debt, it is likely that the lender will file a lawsuit against you.

The long-term effects of bankruptcy

In order to make a decision about whether bankruptcy is right for you, you also need to focus on the long-term effects. The first, and most significant of the effects, is on your credit report. Each of your lenders reports if you pay your bills on time and the amount you owe to a credit-reporting agency, commonly called a credit bureau. All of the information reported then goes into a complex algorithm that determines what your credit score is. The credit bureaus only provide basic information on how they calculate your credit score to avoid anyone trying to manipulate the system. This number follows you throughout your financial life. This collective record of all of your credit usage helps other creditors determine if they will lend money to you. It also has other effects:

- Employers may consult your credit report to determine if you are a responsible person based solely on your credit score.

- If you plan to buy a home, you need a good credit score. Some lenders have increased their requirements for credit scores to higher levels due to the number of fore-closures they have had.

- Some insurance agencies base the rates they charge you for automobile, home, and other insurance on your credit score. Those who have a poor credit score may be more of a risk.

As you can see, your credit report is one of the most important financial tools you have. However, bankruptcy will negatively affect it: Your credit score will drop to very low levels. The type of bankruptcy you are filing determines the length it will remain on your credit report, but this is usually between seven and ten years. During this period, it will be harder to qualify for loans. However, you may be able to get new lines of credit after a few years of hard work rebuilding your credit.

For some, there is a social stigma attached to bankruptcy, too. This has changed somewhat in the last few years, especially as more people file for bankruptcy. Still, for some, bankruptcy is an admittance of failure. There is no specific need to tell family and friends about what you are going through. However, when you file for bankruptcy, a public record of this action takes place. Anyone who looks for this information in legal court documents can find it.

Making the Decision to File for Bankruptcy

With the knowledge now gained about debt management and other options, will you still need to file for bankruptcy? Making this decision is not easy — it can be one of the most difficult decisions you make— and it will affect you for the rest of your life.

First, consider your need to file for bankruptcy. If you have exhausted all other ways to repay your debts or they are not applicable to you, it may be time to file for bankruptcy. For many people with extensive debt, there is no other option for repayment.

Next, consider your current state of well-being. If you are physically and emotionally exhausted from repaying your debts or struggling to do so, bankruptcy can help. Bankruptcy gives you a new lease on financial health by erasing debts, which will translate into improvements in stress levels for many people. The physical strain of owing money could be causing you to work too much or to avoid dealing with health consequences.

Finally, consider what could happen if you do file for bankruptcy. Not only is your debt erased, but you can also start working on building a stronger financial life. This may mean that you will be able to build up your wealth, put money away for savings, and may even help to get better loans in the long term. Consider these stress reliefs a bit further.

Although the effects of filing for bankruptcy are extreme when it comes to your credit report, maintaining your current debt load without repayment could be just as bad. If it will take you 10 years to repay your debt, and during that time, you will consistently make late payments and face costly setbacks financially because of the debt, you are no better off by holding onto your debt. Filing for bankruptcy could mean being free from your debt within a few months. After that, you can continue to build your wealth rather than struggling to pay down your debt.

For those who are concerned about the moral consequences of not repaying the debt discharged in bankruptcy, there is nothing to worry about. Some individuals feel they have a moral obligation to do so because they made a promise to lenders they would repay what was borrowed when they agreed to the loan. After you file for bankruptcy, such as Chapter 7 discharge, you are no longer legally required to repay your debt. However, you can still do so. You can still make payments to your lenders to pay off the loan in full, if you would like to do so. In addition, filing for bankruptcy reorganization does not wipe out any of your debt, but restructures it. For those concerned about the implications of not repaying their debt, such as the religious beliefs you may have, consider filing for Chapter 11, 12, or 13 instead of Chapter 7.

Now that you understand the basics of bankruptcy, the next thing you will do is to consider how to work through the process. Here is a general outline of the steps you will take:

1. Make the decision to file.
2. Work with an attorney to determine your eligibility.
3. Work through consumer credit counseling, if necessary.

4. File all documentation with the bankruptcy court.
5. Attend a bankruptcy meeting.
6. Wait to learn if your debt has been discharged.

This is a very broad description of the bankruptcy process, but each element is explained in the coming chapters at length.

As mentioned, there are numerous types of bankruptcy. In order to make this process easier to understand, the remainder of this book is divided into two sections, one for personal bankruptcy (ideal for consumers) and one for businesses (small to medium-sized businesses). Take a closer look at your options for filing for bankruptcy; *Section 1 explains consumer bankruptcy, and Section 2 details the bankruptcy process for small businesses.* You may realize that this process is not as difficult to work through as you may have thought. A lack of knowledge keeps many people unaware of what bankruptcy has to offer.

PART 1

Consumer Bankruptcy

As an individual, filing for bankruptcy can change your life for the better by simply freeing you from your burden of debt. In this section of the book, we will work through the options available to consumers who are considering filing bankruptcy. We will look at both Chapter 7 and Chapter 13 bankruptcies.

Although each person's situation is different, only the facts are provided here. With the aid of an attorney, determine if filing bankruptcy is right for your individual circumstance.

CHAPTER 2

THE RIGHT TYPE OF CONSUMER BANKRUPTCY

Consumers, or non-business owners, file for bankruptcy under one of two different chapters: Chapter 7 and Chapter 13. Before you decide which you should file, you need to understand the implications of each, as well as how they will affect your debt. The most significant difference between the two is what happens with the debt. In Chapter 7 bankruptcy, debt is discharged, which means you no longer have to repay that debt; it is no longer your legal responsibility. Any assets you own that are not exempt may be sold, but some secured debts you may want to keep. Nevertheless, most of this debt is not repaid. In Chapter 13 bankruptcy, the debt is reorganized with the help of a bankruptcy trustee to make repayment easier. You will repay the debt over a period of three to five years. By showing the court you are unable to repay your debt, you are able to file for Chapter 7, though those who are able to repay debt are usually required to file Chapter 13.

Consumer bankruptcy allows you to get back in control of your finances, but it is not an easy decision to make. Each type of bankruptcy must be filed according to the procedures under bankruptcy law, usually with the help of an attorney. Also, keep in mind that bankruptcy laws do change whenever Congress decides there is a need. You will need to remain up to date when filing. Take a closer look at how these two types of bankruptcy relate to your situation.

Total Discharge in Chapter 7 Bankruptcy

When most people think of bankruptcy, they are thinking of Chapter 7 bankruptcy. This type of bankruptcy is **straight bankruptcy**, in which a bankruptcy filer's assets are liquidated to repay the debts held by lenders, and any debt that is valued higher than assets is discharged. It is the most popular type of bankruptcy filed, because it gives individuals a clean slate from which to rebuild their financial life.

First off, keep in mind that not all types of debts can be discharged. Before determining if you qualify for bankruptcy otherwise, realize that student loan debt, recent tax debt and alimony/ child support are not eligible for discharge. You will need to repay these debts.

Before you can count on Chapter 7 bankruptcy to improve your financial situation, be sure you qualify for it. In short, bankruptcy may not be available for everyone, especially if the bankruptcy courts determine that you have the financial means either to repay your debt as it stands or to repay the debt under a reorganization plan. For those who have followed the changes in bankruptcy law, you may be wondering about this adjustment. Under

the original bankruptcy laws, you could choose the type of bankruptcy you wanted to file without facing limitations. Most people
selected Chapter 7 for its easy solution to debt. However, under
the new bankruptcy laws established in 2005, some people have
no choice in the type of bankruptcy available to them. Why the
change? The new law was created to ensure that people who have
the financial ability to repay their debt do so by reorganizing that
debt under Chapter 13 bankruptcy. Credit lenders often felt that
too many people were taking the solution of liquidation because
it was simpler and the ramifications were easier to overcome.
However, unless you qualify for Chapter 7 bankruptcy, this decision is now out of the filer's hands.

Rather than making the decision yourself, it is now up to the U.S.
bankruptcy trustee who oversees your case to determine the type
of bankruptcy you will file. The bankruptcy trustee's job is to liquidate any assets you may have to get creditors the most money
they can have, while ensuring that you follow the proper steps to
filing for bankruptcy. Ultimately, if you do qualify for Chapter 7
bankruptcy, you can determine if you wish to file Chapter 13 over
Chapter 7, though few people will do this, simply because getting
out of debt through discharge is the better financial decision for
them. Most who qualify for Chapter 7 bankruptcy simply want
their debt discharged because it is too difficult to repay. Based
on your debts and income, the trustee determines your financial
ability. The decision of the U.S. trustee is based on income, debts,
and the daily living expenses you have as well as the information
provided in bankruptcy paperwork. If eligible, your attorney can
often help you make the right decision between Chapter 7 and
Chapter 13 bankruptcy, based on the limitations and laws regarding filing Chapter 7.

Your current, average monthly income is one factor in determining if you are eligible to file for Chapter 7 bankruptcy. To determine what your average monthly income is, add up your income over the last six months and divide by six. Then, compare the figure you come up with to the median family income in your state. This information is available through your local bankruptcy court. You may be eligible to file Chapter 7 bankruptcy if your income is lower than the median income for your state. If you calculate your average monthly income and find it is over the median family income for your state, you may not qualify to file for Chapter 7 bankruptcy; Chapter 13 bankruptcy may be your only filing choice. You do have the option of not filing at all, as well.

There are other tools, however, which can help you qualify for Chapter 7 bankruptcy even if your income is too high. You will need to take a means test to find out if you qualify otherwise. This test compares what your income is and what your expenses are. Then, it considers how much debt you have and your ability to pay off some of your unsecured debts. If the test shows you have enough income to pay off some of your debt, a Chapter 13 repayment plan may be the route you have to take, instead of Chapter 7 bankruptcy.

If your income is too high for you to qualify for Chapter 7 bankruptcy but your means test shows you do not have enough disposable income, in relation to your expenses, to be successful with a Chapter 13 repayment plan, Chapter 7 bankruptcy may still be an option. Further, a means test demonstrates to the bankruptcy court that you do have a real need to file for bankruptcy and are not trying to abuse the system. The trustee is then likely to allow your case to be filed as a Chapter 7 bankruptcy. Your attorney can help you to find out if Chapter 7 bankruptcy is something you qualify for. An attorney will be able to work through bankruptcy documents and help you determine if your case will make it through the system, or if you should consider a Chapter 13 plan. If you are working with an experienced attorney, he or she will know what the chances of success are.

Once you have passed the means test and determined you can file Chapter 7 bankruptcy, the process can continue. You will file documentation with the courts citing what your debts are, and you will also explain your income and expenses in a typical month. All this documentation is submitted to the appointed trustee, who will determine the next steps. In most cases, your Chapter 7 bankruptcy case will process within three months. It will cost about $300 (though costs do change) to file your case. You will need to have these funds to file your bankruptcy documents. Your attorney may charge an additional amount as well. Once payments happen, the case officially goes to bankruptcy court.

At court, you will have to meet with the judge in the case for a short session. The judge will ask questions about why you are filing for bankruptcy and what led you to this point. After this, your information is compiled, and then you start waiting. Generally, within the next three months, you will find out if your case has been discharged. When your case is labeled as discharged, this means that the debts included in the Chapter 7 have been cleared from your responsibility and no longer need to be repaid. It is rare that a bankruptcy would not be discharged. If this happens, it may be caused by a failure to provide adequate information to the court, missing deadlines, or not being truthful about your assets. Once you receive official word that your case has been discharged, you no longer have to repay the debts you owe.

However, there are consequences to filing Chapter 7 bankruptcy that can be worse than filing Chapter 13. Though lenders cannot come after you legally, most will not lend to you again. More so, it will be harder to qualify for any loans or lines of credit, especially in the two years after your discharge date, because lenders will see your poor past performance in managing your debt. After a few years, many lenders are willing to extend a small credit limit to you to allow you to prove your ability to manage debt has improved.

Eventually lenders may be willing to lend to you again, but that depends on how well your handle your money up until that time. Bankruptcy will remain on your credit report for up to ten years. Throughout that entire time, you will have a much more difficult time obtaining credit. When you do qualify for credit, lenders are likely to charge you more in finance charges than others would pay because of this black mark on your report. However, if you have been unable to pay your debt, but decide not to file bankruptcy, you are likely to face the same problem continuously.

Reorganization in Chapter 13 Bankruptcy

Although many people would prefer to file Chapter 7 bankruptcy because it dismisses debt from having to be paid, it is not always the best option. It may not be a possibility, either, if the U.S. trustee finds that your income is sufficient to pay a portion or all of your debt. Chapter 13 is unique in that you are not able to completely wipe off the slate and start over. You will work to put a plan in place to repay your debt over a period of time, eventually paying off most of what you owe.

Chapter 13 bankruptcy also has limitations and qualifications. In order to file a bankruptcy of this type, your income needs to be lower than the median family income, or it needs to be substantially less than your monthly expenses. In situations where your family's income is higher than your state's median and you have excess funds compared to your expenses, filing for bankruptcy will not be an option. Rather, the lenders will be able to force you to repay your debts, in the way that they have already established through the agreements you signed with them, such as garnishing your wages or filing a lien on your property. However, most people who need to file for Chapter 13 bankruptcy are able to do so without difficulty, assuming their expenses and income align properly. Specifically, those who have the income to repay their debts will be required to repay those debts as the court prescribes. It is likely that some debts will be discharged, such as credit card debts, up to a certain point depending on the amount of income available. The bankruptcy trustee determines this based on your income and expenses plus the amount of debt you are filing for bankruptcy for. Most people can get help through this reorganization plan, because it allows the debt to be reorganized into manageable payments.

With Chapter 13 bankruptcy, individuals will go through the basic initial steps of filing bankruptcy paperwork, *which will be discussed in Chapter 3*. However, the U.S. trustee will help you establish a payment plan with your creditors. This plan is created to do several key things for you, as the filer:

- It stops any foreclosures or liens occurring on your property immediately, though these may later go through, depending on the court's reorganization plan.

- It stops creditors from harassing you through phone calls and usually halts creditors' ability to file or pursue lawsuits against you.

- It may reduce your debts owed, depending on the type of debt. Unsecured debt, such as credit cards, may be reduced rather than repaid in full.

- It allows you to keep all assets that you own (assuming you meet your payment requirements), even after the bankruptcy plan has gone through.

The ultimate goal of Chapter 13 is to establish a repayment plan you submit with the help of your attorney. The plan you create needs to show that you can repay all of your mandatory debts and at least some of the other debt you have over the next three to five years. At the time you start the plan, you need to show you earn enough income to pay your debts monthly without falling behind on payments. Specifically, you have to prove that you can remain current on any secured collateral debts (mortgages or car loans) you have, which you want to keep. You also need to show that you can stay up to date on payments of back taxes, child support payments, or any other secured debt while you make your current payments. In addition to this, the repayment plan must also show that you will make all payments on the unsecured debt you have, up to the value of the nonexempt property. "Nonexempt property" is any type of asset that could be lost through a total discharge of debt through Chapter 7 bankruptcy. For example, if you plan to repay a loan you received to buy a computer, you must have the ability to repay that loan up to the value of the computer purchased.

The comprehensive reorganization plan shows the bankruptcy court you can and will repay your debts, though it may be in a different way than you have been paying them up until this point. If you do not have disposable income that would allow you to repay the debts included in your plan, the bankruptcy trustee determines which debts and how much of each will be repaid. Those debts based on assets, such as your home and vehicle, are often repaid in full or the asset is confiscated to repay the debt. In some cases, you will need to repay all of the debt you owe to a lender, such as with secured debts. In others, you may not have to repay any of the debt at all, or may pay a small portion, especially if you do not have enough disposable income to pay all unsecured debts. This includes unsecured debt, such as credit cards and personal loans. When you took out these loans, lenders understood an asset was not in place to secure the loans and, therefore, no assets have to be used to repay the debt if you default on them.

Within the Chapter 13 bankruptcy repayment plan, you must outline how you will repay those debts that are required to be repaid, such as back taxes, child support, and secured debts (like mortgages). In addition, if you have disposable income after these debts are paid, you must show in the plan how you will pay down unsecure debts. Once you have a plan organized and ready for the trustee to read, you will submit it through your attorney to the trustee. The trustee will approve the plan assuming that it clearly outlines your plan to pay off your debts. If the trustee does not approve the plan, it goes back to you to be reworked so it is a feasible plan for repaying the debt. If approved, then it moves on to the bankruptcy court judge. The judge looks at the details of the plan, determines if the plan is executable, and then determines if the plan accounts for payment of every creditor entitled to a claim. A judge may rule that you do not have to repay your credit card lenders back if you do not have the disposable income to do so. There is not a specific list of what gets paid back first, though. The judge may even rule that you do have to repay some lenders if he or she believes you can do so based on your income and expenses. Often, any amount of money you can repay will be divided between lenders.

If the judge approves the claim, the repayment period is established. This period generally lasts between three and five years, and you will make monthly payments according to the plan over this time. You do not lose your assets during this time, but you do have to monitor your spending and credit use, because the courts will be looking at this information very closely. After the repayment period is over, you have satisfied all of your debts and can move on with your financial life. After a Chapter 13 bankruptcy discharge, a notification of your bankruptcy will remain on your credit report for the next seven years, which occurs after you make the final payment in your plan. The next few years will be the most difficult in terms of obtaining credit, because it is likely that lenders will be concerned about the risk they are taking by lending to you.

However, Chapter 13 bankruptcy is not worse than filing Chapter 7 bankruptcy; in many cases, it is better. By repaying your lenders, even over a longer period, you are showing your responsibility to them. You are demonstrating that you are willing to meet your agreements, even if you cannot do so immediately. Because many debts are unpaid to their full level through this type of bankruptcy, though, it may be some time until lenders are confident enough to give you a new credit card or line of credit. The amount of time this takes is dependent on how well you work to rebuild your credit after filing for bankruptcy. Chapter 7 immediately causes your credit score to fall, and it will remain that way for some time, while Chapter 13 bankruptcy may allow your score to improve faster. *More information on rebuilding your credit is found in Chapter 6.*

Keep in mind that most debts can be reorganized into a Chapter 13 plan, including those debts unable to be discharged, such as taxes and student loan payments. Any debts you need to repay are factored into this plan to ensure you repay all of your obligations.

Making Your Bankruptcy Choice

Now that you know the basics about each type of personal bankruptcy, the next step is to dive in and make a decision. It is OK if you are not ready just yet; this is a big decision to make, and therefore, you should consider some of the pros and cons of each type of bankruptcy before you make a decision.

With personal bankruptcy in Chapter 7, you are able to get rid of your debt faster. Rather than spending three to five years repaying your debt and being under the watchful eye of the U.S. trustee, you can be working on rebuilding your credit. In fact, three years after your discharge from Chapter 7, many creditors will issue limited forms of credit to users, which may be secured credit lines that are backed by a deposit you make. Some may offer low credit-limit credit cards, too. You may even qualify for a new mortgage loan. If you filed Chapter 13 instead, you would still find yourself in the midst of repayments after three years.

On the other hand, due to having too much disposable income, there are many people who will no longer qualify to repay their debt under the traditional Chapter 7 bankruptcy. Be sure to work with your attorney closely if you are unsure if you can qualify for Chapter 7. There are circumstances where a bankruptcy judge will be lenient with Chapter 7 qualifications, and a bankruptcy attorney should help you through this process of getting qualified if it is possible to do so. Take a closer look at yourself and the goals that you have established for your future financial stability. The following tips can help you gauge what your decision should be:

- **If you file Chapter 7 bankruptcy and all of your debts disappear in three months, will you have learned your lesson?** For some people, this easy method of getting out of repaying credit cards only leads to further abuse of them. In a few years, you could be right back in the same place you are right now, struggling with debt.

- **Do you need to make any significant purchases in the next three years?** A Chapter 13 bankruptcy filing prohibits you from making significant purchases over the repayment period. Any substantial purchase made, such as a home or a vehicle, must be approved by the U.S. trustee before you can make the purchase. You also will be limited to the amount of credit you can use during your repayment period. Generally, you will want to close all credit lines. However, some people elect to keep some in good standing open. Keep any purchases or usage of credit less than $1,000 to avoid drawing the attention of the trustee. Be sure you can repay the money borrowed within the month, too.

- **Are you confident you can maintain your repayment plan throughout the period?** If you fail your Chapter 13 repayment plan, such as missing payments you have agreed to, the lenders do have the right to sue you for those payments. You may lose your home if you get behind again on your mortgage, or you may be required to make payments in the form of garnishments. Unless you keep up your repayment plan, the case may receive dismissal in a court of law, giving all lenders the ability to seek full payment from you again.

- **Are you prepared to lose any assets you own that are not exempt?** In Chapter 7 bankruptcy, you could lose your possessions. Remember that in many situations, non-exempt assets will need to be sold or returned to the lender to repay your debts. If you have too much equity in your home, you may need to sell it. If you have expensive electronics or jewelry, you may lose these items.

- **In the next three to five years, do you plan to send a child off to college with a loan you fund?** Do you plan to make significant investments, start a business, or otherwise have a substantial amount of money made available to you through creditors? If so, a fast discharge through Chapter 7 may be the route to take. On the other hand, it may be too risky to consider bankruptcy at all if you know you will need good credit in a short amount of time.

It is critical to think of all of the good and bad aspects of filing for bankruptcy before filling. It is not easy to make this decision, but it will be something you have to deal with for the next ten years. During that time, you could face significant limitations on credit use, including mortgage loans or car loans. For example, you may find your insurance company will charge you more because of your poor credit history.

Your bankruptcy attorney

The decision to file for bankruptcy is often made with the help of an attorney. An attorney is not required to file for bankruptcy, because most of the bankruptcy courts provide self-help information and tutorials on their Web sites and at offices. However, most people will want to pay the small fee to use the services of a qualified professional to ensure the process is carried out smoothly and correctly.

Hiring a bankruptcy attorney is often the best decision an individual who is filing for bankruptcy will make, and the reasons are simple. They have the experience and the ability to get your bankruptcy through the courts in the most efficient way with a reduced chance of the case being thrown out. It is important to keep in mind that, although you have the legal right to file for bankruptcy, you must meet specific qualifications and procedural steps to make it happen, including submitting the proper paperwork and adhering to a schedule provided by the courts. If you fail to do this, the bankruptcy court will throw your case out, leaving you without the ability to get rid of your debt. You will need to wait at least six months before reapplying for bankruptcy if this happens. Look for the following specific qualities in the bankruptcy attorney you hire:

- **Hire an attorney licensed in your state**. Verify the license or locate an attorney through the state's bar association.

- **Hire an attorney who specializes in bankruptcy law**. This individual will be the most up to date on the changes in the laws and will be able to work with you to meet any specific requirements.

- **Find an attorney that you trust and like**. You will be working with your attorney on various occasions. You will need this professional to have the ability to answer your questions and to interact with you easily. If you do not trust him or her, how will you tell the attorney the intimate details of your finances?

- **Look for a bankruptcy attorney who fits your particular needs.** Many offer payment plans to make paying for their services and the filing fee as easy as possible. They also provide you with resources to help make the right decision, without forcing a decision on you. Some attorneys are popular in local areas because of their abilities to work well with their clients. Ask for referrals from family and friends, so long as this process is not something you want to keep from them.

Once you have hired the attorney, the next step in the process is to work through this person; use him or her as the middleman. Your bankruptcy attorney will handle virtually all of the claims you make. The initial meeting is often an opportunity to discuss your options, so bring your debt information with you, as well as an idea of typical monthly income and expenses. Your attorney is not there to judge you, but he or she will be able to take this information and determine if you qualify for bankruptcy.

The initial meeting is often an opportunity to discuss the costs of filing and your ability to file. The attorney will then determine the next steps based on if you can file for Chapter 7 or Chapter 13. In many situations, you (the filer) will be setting in place the next steps, meaning you will be setting up a payment plan with your attorney and scheduling a time to file the case based on your specific needs. Your attorney will give you documents to fill out including a **debtor's sheet**, which lists your debts and the lenders who hold them. In Chapter 7 bankruptcy filings the attorney is responsible for administering a means test, if it is necessary to do so based on your income and the amount of debt you are filing. This will determine if your expenses are higher than your income to the point that you qualify for Chapter 7 bankruptcy. Financial counseling services, as needed, may occur with the help of your attorney. If you are filing Chapter 13 bankruptcy, your attorney will help you to construct a repayment plan based on your debts and help you to find credit-counseling services, if needed.

The next time you meet with your attorney, you will need to sign your documentation to file for bankruptcy. This process only takes a few minutes, but it can be a bit overwhelming, because you are formally committing to a bankruptcy decision. After this binding step has taken place, you will next meet with your attorney to attend the creditor's meeting, which is an opportunity for you to state your case in front of a judge. Your attorney will guide you through the process and, after this point, it is in the hands of the bankruptcy courts. If your case is discharged, or your Chapter 13 repayment plan is accepted, you will not likely be in contact with your attorney again, unless there are specific questions that you have. For example, you may ask your attorney questions about the progress of the case or ask questions about the consequences of the court's actions.

The hiring of an attorney is a big decision. Although it costs anywhere from a few hundred dollars up to a couple of thousand dollars, the knowledge and guidance an experienced attorney offers you is unmatched. You do have the ability to file for bankruptcy without the help of an attorney, but it is not recommended due to the complexities of the filing process.

"Most people should not try to file the [bankruptcy] case themselves. There is a class of consumer debtor with a very simple factual situation that could safely file their own case, with proper instructions. But any complication or combination of factors, or even one significant issue, could make that an unwise decision."
—Rick West, practicing attorney

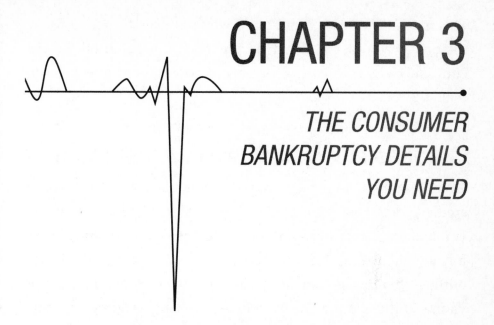

CHAPTER 3

THE CONSUMER BANKRUPTCY DETAILS YOU NEED

Now that you have a solid understanding of what consumer bankruptcy options you have, it is time to focus on the actual process. Most people will not make a decision about filing for bankruptcy until they know what is likely to happen in the process. You might have made the decision to file for bankruptcy but might still be unsure about how the process works. Although some details of the bankruptcy process were previously mentioned, it is important to understand the details and logistics thoroughly.

At the time of publication, the latest laws put in place in 2005 have tightened the procedures for filing for bankruptcy. The goal is to ensure that only those who truly need to file for bankruptcy — those who are not abusing the system — get the best opportunity to do so. Creditors have more ability to file complaints and legal suits in bankruptcy now to help ensure that their opinions are heard. If a creditor brings such a complaint to the court, during the creditors' meeting, the court determines if the creditor's complaints are valid and makes a decision on how to proceed.

This may affect if you can file or if you will be required to repay the debt. Each case is decided independently based on the circumstances of your case. However, it is rare for creditors to do this.

Credit is a Legal, Binding Agreement

To look at the bankruptcy process closer, consider the standard credit card agreement. If you read the fine print of the agreement, you will see it specifically outlines a few important points. These include the costs and fees associated with owning the card. It also outlines that the agreement you are making — by accepting, activating, and using the line of credit — is legally binding, and you are agreeing to repay the money you borrow.

What does that mean to you now? In a court of law, a contract or other legally binding agreement is proof that someone has specific rights to enforce what was decided upon in the agreement. In this case, the creditor has the right to make you pay back the money you borrowed, according to the terms of the agreement. With this in mind, remember that during bankruptcy, you are asking a judge to put aside such an agreement and to side with you in erasing your debt: That is not a small decision to make. The judge needs to ensure that the financial circumstances you are in were unavoidable and that you have no other way out.

The new laws enacted in 2005 help to establish some legal ground for lenders. In fact, you will attend a creditors' meeting. This meeting is an opportunity for your creditors to come forward and even be part of the meeting — although it is rare for them to do so. They may ask the judge to rule on their behalf and not write off the debt you have accumulated. The creditors may make their case about why you should have to pay that debt back, such as making claims that you took on the loan knowing you could not repay it. Again, it is rare that creditors actually attend this meeting because most personal bankruptcies are small change and not worth the investment of the company to hire an attorney to make these claims. However, keep in mind that the creditor should receive repayment of the borrowed funds whenever it is possible for the borrower to do so, through one method or the other. This is the opinion of the bankruptcy judge in most cases. As you proceed to file for bankruptcy, be sure your entire case establishes that you have no means to repay your debt (in cases of Chapter 7 bankruptcy) and that you are not abusing the system by filing.

Eligibility to File for Bankruptcy

You have debt, and you are struggling to repay that debt. You may think this is all it takes to qualify for bankruptcy, but that is not the way that the U. S. federal government understands it. Rather, the government wants to be sure you are not abusing the system by ensuring that any funds that can be repaid are indeed repaid rather than written off.

Assuming you are just considering bankruptcy at this point rather than debt consolidation or debt settlement, the first step in filing for bankruptcy is to determine if you can make repayment through a Chapter 13 plan. Your attorney and the trustee will weigh this question, too. Anyone who can make payment, even over five years, may need to file Chapter 13 bankruptcy instead of Chapter 7. *To find out more about Chapter 7 and Chapter 13 bankruptcies, see Chapter 2.*

Will the court allow you to discharge all of your debt through Chapter 7? Will the court convert your Chapter 7 to a Chapter 13 instead? The following sections discuss the process of determining which type of bankruptcy the court will allow you to file.

Determining if a Chapter 13 repayment plan is a possibility

The first step to determine eligibility to file for bankruptcy is to find out if you have the income to repay your debt through a Chapter 13 repayment plan rather than filing Chapter 7 bankruptcy. Under bankruptcy laws, those with a higher income may be unable to file Chapter 7 bankruptcy. A U.S. trustee may decide that you can repay your debts, or some of your debts, through reorganization of that debt if your income is higher than the median family income or your expenses are significantly lower than your income.

Calculate current monthly income

Your legal monthly income is the average monthly income over a period of six months prior to the month you filed for bankruptcy. Your income includes all forms of income received, including taxable and not taxable income. Calculate your income using your gross income before taxes are withdrawn from your paycheck. If you were unemployed within the six months prior to filing for bankruptcy, your monthly income may be skewed. If you worked for the first three months, for example, but not for the second three months, your average income is not a clear representation of what your current income is because you did not earn a consistent, stable income. Nevertheless, you need to provide this average income when filing for bankruptcy, even if it is not an accurate representation of what your income is now. How can this affect your eligibility to file? If you only worked for three months of those six months and your average income is higher than your state's median family income, this could result in ineligibility, even if your income right now is nothing. That is simply how the system works, so it may be best to wait a few months to ensure this is not the case.

To calculate your income, gather your financial documents. Add together all of the money you were paid in the six months before you plan to file for bankruptcy. Divide this number by six, for six months. This tells you your monthly average over that six-month period. In calculating all of your income, you need to factor in:

- All income from wages, salaries, bonuses, overtime payments, tips, and commissions.

- Gross income from any business that you are operating (income from a farm or other profession).

- All rent monies and other income derived from rental properties.

- All interest, royalties, and dividends from investments or other.

- All pensions and retirement income received (though you do not have to use retirement funds that are not being withdrawn).

- All contributions from your spouse if he or she is not filing for bankruptcy with you. When only one spouse is filing for bankruptcy, any income given to the filer from the non-filing spouse must be included.

- All contributions for household expenses made by another person, including child support, spousal support, or other contributions (this includes all contributions made to you on behalf of your dependents).

- All state disability insurance you have received.

- All annuity payments you have received.

- All unemployment compensation you have received.

- All workers compensation payments received.

- Any type of lump sum or windfall payment, including lottery winnings or other funds.

You do not have to report income from payments you receive that come under the Social Security Act, which includes Social Security retirement benefits, Social Security Disability Insurance, Supplemental Security Income, or Temporary Assistance for Needy Families. It may be possible not to include your state unemployment insurance, depending on the laws within your state. You also do not have to include any payments made to you as compensation as a victim of domestic terrorism, war crimes, or crimes against humanity.

If you fail to report any information accurately, the court could dismiss your bankruptcy case. This may stop you from filing for bankruptcy now and potentially in the future, especially if it is believed that you were abusing the system.

Compare your state's family median income to your own

Now that you know what your monthly income is, the next step in the process is to compare this information to your state's family median income. To gather this information, you need only to turn to the U.S. Census Bureau. Each year, the census bureau publishes the annual family median income for each of the 50 states. You can find the current numbers for your state by visiting the U.S. Trustee Program at **www.justice.gov/ust**. There, you will click on the link that says "Means Testing Information." Remember: This is an annual income rather than a monthly income. You will need to divide the state's income figure by 12 to get the monthly income, and compare the figure to your current monthly income.

Though not always the case, many people will find their income is either at or less than their state's median. If this is the case, you are likely to be able to file Chapter 7 bankruptcy. In addition, you will find that your actual monthly income and your actual expenses (as opposed to your current income figures over a six-month period) may also have some affect on your ability to file Chapter 7 bankruptcy. If you find that your income does exceed what your state lists as the median, this is a signal to the court that you may or may not qualify for bankruptcy. You will then need to take the means test. This is a process of determining what your actual circumstances are on a more personalized basis. The goal is to find out if you are trying to abuse the system or if you honestly need to file bankruptcy. You need to tell the court about any special circumstances that make your debt difficult to repay. The means test helps the court discover those circumstances.

Taking a means test

Your attorney may conduct the means test or, if you are filing for bankruptcy on your own, you will need to use Form 22A of the bankruptcy forms called the Statement of Current Monthly Income and Means Test Calculation, which is available through the U.S. Courts Web site or some third party providers. This form is lengthy and resembles a tax form in the way it is laid out. The form outlines your income and expenses in detail to clearly show where your money is going each month. You will enter income information and follow specific instructions for calculating each of the steps. Detailed instructions are provided with the form. If you do complete this on your own (and it is not advisable to do so without your attorney, to ensure accuracy) you will turn it in to the bankruptcy trustee to determine if your expenses and income are considered non-abusive of bankruptcy. If you fail the means test, you may still qualify for a Chapter 7 bankruptcy if you have specific, approved special circumstances, depending on the ruling of the trustee. An example of a special circumstance may be having excessive income to pay for a disabled child. Although your income is higher than the state's median family income, the higher income is necessary to care for your child. The trustee will note this as not being abusive of bankruptcy laws, based on the information you provide in your means test.

If you do not pass the means test in the eyes of the trustee, the case is labeled as **presumed abuse**. If your case receives a label as presumed abuse, you will not be able to proceed unless you can prove the presumption of abuse should be overlooked because of special circumstances. This process of reviewing the potential abusive behavior is not automatic. In order to stop your case on the presumption of abuse, someone must file a complaint that it is abusive. A creditor, the trustee, or the U.S. trustee may do this. The U.S. trustee is not working directly with you but oversees the bankruptcy court trustee that is working on you particular case. The U.S. trustee receives your case after it is presented to the court and will likely be the one to file the complaint.

To file a complaint, a request for a court hearing must be filed to dismiss or to convert the case to a Chapter 13 bankruptcy. The U.S. trustee will need to file a statement within ten days after you have the meeting of creditors, to indicate whether the case should be considered presumed abusive. The U.S. trustee will file a complaint of this kind when your income is more than the state median. Within five days from the filing of this statement, the U.S. trustee's statement then goes to all of your creditors. This process is to inform the creditors of the presumed abusive decision and to give the creditors the opportunity to file a motion to dismiss or to convert the case. After 30 days of the filing of this statement, the U.S. trustee must then do one of two things. The trustee may dismiss the case because he or she believes that you are abusing the system, or he or she may convert the case for the same reason. The trustee also has the option of stating why dismissing the case is not necessary. For example, if you were able to pass the means test, this is a reason not to dismiss the case. The trustee must either file his or her own motion to convert or dismiss the case on the grounds of abuse or explain why a motion to convert or dismiss the case is not appropriate. One reason the second option may be used is because you passed the means test.

These specific timeframes and details only apply to the U.S. trustee. Any of your creditors can file a motion to dismiss or convert at any time during your filing if your income is higher than the state median. However, they do not have the ability to file such a motion after 60 days of the first date set for your meeting of creditors.

Handling a motion to dismiss or convert

The court may dismiss your case, which means that it may throw it out of bankruptcy court. The court may decide that you have the means to repay some of your debt and will then convert it to a Chapter 13 bankruptcy instead of Chapter 7. If, at any time during this process, you find that a creditor or the U.S. trustee has filed a motion to dismiss or convert your case to a Chapter 13 repayment plan, you do have options. If a claim like this occurs, you are entitled to a notice of the hearing at least 20 days prior to the date of the hearing. You will receive documentation in the mail, which details why the action was filed as well as what you need to do to respond to the motion. In this situation, it is up to you to prove to the court that your filing of Chapter 7 bankruptcy is not abusive and that it should be allowed to stand.

How will you accomplish this? Though your attorney can guide you through the process and provide you with specifics on your case, two basic defenses may be used:

1.   **You did not fail the means test**: If you have completed Form 22A and it shows you did in fact pass the means test, you will need to show this to the court. In some cases, there may be some level of confusion as to the state's laws regarding specific types of income. For example, if your state does not allow social security income to be included in your income allotment, your creditors may have filed a claim to dismiss because they did include this information. In either case, you must show that you did pass the means test and that your creditors (or other body) are mistaken.

2. **There are special circumstances that should allow you to pass the means test**: Under the current bankruptcy laws, there is terminology for special circumstances, though these are not specifically defined. The law does specifically list medical conditions or a call to active duty in the armed forces to be special circumstances for filing Chapter 7 bankruptcy. However, this is not an exhaustive list.

If you have some special circumstance that you believe is a reason to be able to file Chapter 7 bankruptcy, you must show what that circumstance is and you must justify any additional expenses or adjustments to your current monthly income. The law states that you must show that there is no reasonable alternative; you need to show you had no other choice.

If you want to show that you have such special circumstances, you need to follow a specific method. Present an itemized list of each of the additional expenses you have or the adjustments to your income that you make. You will need to show proof of these expenses and adjustments by providing documentation of them. Also, provide a detailed explanation of what the circumstances are and why it is necessary for you to have these expenses or adjustments. Further, in order for these special circumstances to be enough for the court to rule you can file Chapter 7 bankruptcy, the additional expenses or adjustments to your income must enable you to pass the means test.

For many people, the process of bankruptcy starts with trying to file Chapter 7 bankruptcy. If you do not qualify for that, then Chapter 13 might be an option for you. Most people will have success filing Chapter 13, unless your income is significantly higher than your expenses and you have the means to repay your debt. If you do not make it through to Chapter 7 bankruptcy, realize that Chapter 13 can provide a variety of benefits, including **automatic stays**, which stop foreclosure and garnishments. It also will stop creditors from harassing you.

Previous bankruptcy filings

The next step for qualifying to file for bankruptcy is to ensure you have not filed in the past. If so, it must be within the legal requirements. One of the reasons for the new bankruptcy laws that went into effect in 2005 was to limit the frequency with which a person may file for bankruptcy. Previous laws allowed individuals to file for bankruptcy every few years, which allowed many to accumulate debt, file for bankruptcy, and then accumulate debt again with little worry because they could simply go bankrupt once more. Under the new laws, however, this is not the case. If you had a Chapter 7 bankruptcy discharged in the last eight years, you cannot file Chapter 7 again. Chapter 13 can be filed every two years, unless the filer has a previous Chapter 7 bankruptcy; in that case, there is a four-year waiting period.

In addition to this, if you have recently tried to file for bankruptcy and your case received dismissal within the previous 180 days, you will not be able to file again. This holds true if you violated a court order in that bankruptcy filing, or if you asked the court to dismiss your case after a creditor asked for some type of relief from the automatic stay that was put in place.

Get the required counseling

Another prerequisite to filing for bankruptcy of any type is to meet the credit counseling requirements. Credit counseling is one of the additions to bankruptcy laws since the 2005 changes. The goal of credit counseling is to help individuals filing for bankruptcy avoid getting back into that position.

You must have obtained counseling services from an approved credit-counseling organization (check your local bankruptcy court Web site for eligible organizations) within the 180 days prior to filing for bankruptcy. The credit counselor will provide you with a certificate of completion, and you must provide this certificate to the bankruptcy court no later than 15 days after you file or at the time you file your bankruptcy documents. The credit counseling you obtain must receive approval by the U.S. trustee's office. This counseling may occur over the phone, over the Internet, or in person.

Credit-counseling services have the goal of helping you repay your debt through a repayment plan. They will work with you to determine if you qualify for a repayment plan — this is not the same plan you will develop for a Chapter 13 repayment plan. Rather, credit counseling is something you need to do before you file for bankruptcy. The goal here is to have you try to repay your debts through a reorganization of those debts. If you fail at this step, filing for bankruptcy may be necessary. The counseling service will determine if consumers are able to repay some, or all, of their debt through a debt management plan and help them to avoid filing for bankruptcy.

However, there are a few things to keep in mind about credit counseling services. If you do sign up, recognize that creditors may or may not work with you. Second, the creditors are able to pull out of the plan at any time and come after you for any remaining debt they believe you can repay. At that point, if you decide to file for Chapter 7 bankruptcy, any money paid to these creditors is money you did not need to spend because the debt would have been discharged. Nevertheless, the laws of bankruptcy now require everyone who is considering filing either chapter of bankruptcy to work through a counseling service, unless you have extraordinary circumstances such as significant medical debt that could not be avoided. This allows you to avoid filing for bankruptcy if there is a chance you can repay your debts outside of bankruptcy court.

If the credit-counseling service believes you may be eligible to develop a plan, you are obligated to cooperate with them in that regard. This plan must then be filed along with your bankruptcy papers with the court to show that you attempted to repay your debts. If this plan looks like it could work, the U.S. trustee then may use this document to determine if they think a Chapter 13 repayment plan is an option for you, even if you are applying for a Chapter 7 bankruptcy. For example, if the credit-counseling agency puts together a budget and repayment plan that seems feasible, the bankruptcy court may rule that you should be able to follow that plan. The underlying goal here is to clearly demonstrate to the credit-counseling agency that you need to file Chapter 7 bankruptcy because you cannot afford a Chapter 13 repayment plan. In some cases, this can be tricky, but the goal of the court is to ensure that those who can afford to repay their debts, or some of those debts, do so.

Most credit-counseling companies do charge a counseling fee — usually between $25 and $50, although this can vary — for their services. However, agencies are required to offer their services regardless of whether you can pay. If you are unable to make a payment to the agency, demonstrate this information to them by stating why you cannot do so. If they fail to accommodate you because of your inability to pay — it has to be obvious you cannot pay their fee — document all of the proceedings and report this to the U.S. trustee by contacting him or her directly. You should inform the agency; it is a legal requirement for them to offer this service at a rate affordable to you.

How to File Your Case

After you have completed all of the steps above to be eligible to file for bankruptcy, the next step is actually making it happen. Yet another of the changes to the bankruptcy laws in 2005 had to do with this filing process. Rather than relying on creditors to come forward and make a claim against your case, the burden of proof is now on your shoulders. This simply means that you have to do the work to convince the bankruptcy court to grant your decision. The number of forms necessary to file has increased, as well as the complexity of these forms. An attorney could make this process easier for you.

You will need to file all required bankruptcy forms, which will be discussed in Chapter 5. In addition, you will need to file a certificate that shows you completed an approved credit-counseling workshop within the last 180 days. You will need to submit your most recent federal tax return or a transcript of the return. You must also submit your wage documentation for the last 60 days. There are fees that must be paid to the bankruptcy court at the time of the filing. At the time of publication, the cost of filing for Chapter 7 bankruptcy was $299 and the cost of filing for Chapter 13 was $274, but that may change. You can petition the court to reduce or eliminate the fee if you do not have the funds necessary to pay it, but keep in mind this is limited to extreme cases of poverty. In addition, you should check with the local bankruptcy court to determine if there are any local forms and requirements needed to pass in order to file. There are official, standardized forms put in place and maintained through the federal government for bankruptcy proceedings. However, your local bankruptcy court may require you to file additional forms, often just clerical forms required for administration.

You can find all of the bankruptcy forms and documents you need, both federal and local forms included, by visiting the U.S. Court's Web site at **www.uscourts.gov/courtlinks**. However, if you are working with a bankruptcy attorney, he or she will provide you with all of the forms you need. All details for filing for bankruptcy are included on those forms, right down to the order of the forms. If you fail to meet specific guidelines included in these forms, miss deadlines, or fail to provide all necessary documentation, your bankruptcy case may be thrown out of court without further consideration. This is yet another of the reasons to work closely with a bankruptcy attorney rather than tackling the process on your own.

The Automatic Stay

You may have plenty of reasons to file for bankruptcy, but one of the key benefits of doing so is to benefit from the automatic stay.

In fact, it is one of the most powerful aspects of the bankruptcy filing. The automatic stay stops creditors right away. It is a court order halting all types of proceedings by creditors, including secured and unsecured creditors. No creditor may file or take action against you from the time that you file your bankruptcy case until your case is settled by the bankruptcy court.

The automatic stay was added to bankruptcy law in 2005 to give debtors a breather from the strain of financial debts. It helps to give you some relief from the pressures that have pushed you to file for bankruptcy in the first place. All contact with creditors must occur through the trustee from that point on. It also adds another benefit: Everything is on hold at this point. That means you are stripping away the ability of the creditor to take your property from you and putting the bankruptcy court in charge of the decision about whether you get to keep your assets. If the trustee determines that you do need to lose some of your assets, he or she decides how the sale of those assets will occur and which of your creditors will get a piece of the value.

Once you file for bankruptcy, this automatic stay goes into effect without any additional application: You do not have to do anything to get this benefit. If any of your creditors contact you after this point, alert your attorney. Most of the time, once a creditor learns you have filed for bankruptcy, he or she will stop calling because the fines and fees for doing so can be significant. The automatic stay stops collections and collection activity from most types of creditors. However, there are exceptions to this rule. The bankruptcy court may approve further collection activity after considering your bankruptcy case. Moreover, the law excludes some types of debts, as mentioned previously. The collection of most types of debts is stopped, however, including any debt collection companies and attorneys contacting you on behalf of their clients. Even lawsuits brought against you from credit card debt and health care bills will stop in most cases. This includes:

- **All credit card debts, medical debts, and attorney fees**: These organizations may not file a lawsuit against you or proceed with pending lawsuits, record liens against any property, report any debt to a credit-reporting agency, or seize any property or income.

- **Public benefits**: Any government agency or entity that is trying to collect over payments of benefits from Medicaid, Social Security insurance, or Temporary Assistance to Needy Families may not do so, nor may they threaten to cease other payments

- **Criminal proceeding debts**: Those who have a case pending against them that can be broken into criminal and debt components will have the debt components of the case suspended, although the criminal proceedings may continue.

- **Liens from the IRS**: Any liens or levies from the IRS specifically may halt, and the IRS may not seize property or income.

- **Foreclosures**: The initial proceedings of foreclosure will stop when you file for bankruptcy; however, there are limitations in some states where final proceedings and notices that are already in place at the time of your filing will be upheld.

- **Utility companies**: Once you file for bankruptcy, the automatic stay goes into effect for utility companies, and they may no longer file claims against you, nor disconnect your services. However, they may require that you pay a deposit within 20 days of filing for bankruptcy for future usage of those utilities. If you fail to provide such a deposit, they may shut off your usage at that point.

There are some types of collection activities that may not apply to the automatic stay. Congress has defined some specific types of debts or proceedings in which the automatic stay is limited. If this occurs, the collection activity of the creditor will then proceed. These activities include the following:

- **Divorce and child support payments**: It is highly unlikely that any proceedings that are caused by your failure to pay child support or divorce payments will be stopped. This includes any type of action to collect child support, alimony, back payments, or those used to determine visitation or custody of a minor child. It also includes any type of support that comes from domestic violence. In addition, if there are garnishments on your wages or on your tax refunds, those payments will not be stopped by filing for bankruptcy.

- **The taxes you owe**: Most of the time, debts owed to the IRS must be repaid. This includes any debts you may owe from a tax audit or because you failed to file a tax return. Tax assessments are not affected by the automatic stay, nor are any tax deficiency notices you may receive from the IRS. Other types of taxes may be factored into a Chapter 13 repayment plan.

- **Loans from pensions**: If you have taken a loan from your pension or other type of retirement account, the automatic stay does not halt these. Generally, the loans are paid back through a withdrawal from your paycheck. These are not stopped when you file for bankruptcy.

If you have a type of debt collection not listed here that you are concerned about, request further information from your bankruptcy attorney. You can also contact your local bankruptcy court for more information.

Although the automatic stay will continue throughout the bankruptcy case for most people, it is possible for you, the bankruptcy filer, to violate the automatic stay resulting in its cancellation. Your actions may cause the debt to be collected in several situations. For example, if you had a bankruptcy case pending within the year prior to filing the current case and the court refuses your request to allow the stay to kick in, it will not. Further, the bankruptcy code has specific deadlines in place you will need to meet in order to proceed with the filings. If you fail to meet these specific deadlines or you fail to follow the specific instructions for filing your bankruptcy case, this too can cause you to lose the protection of the automatic stay. If you find yourself in a situation where the automatic stay may be lost, contact your attorney to find out how your specific case is affected. You do not want to lose the automatic stay benefit if it possible to avoid doing so.

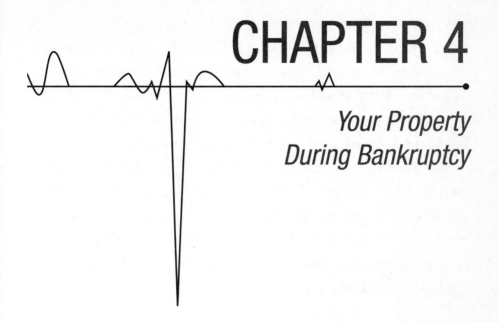

CHAPTER 4

*Your Property
During Bankruptcy*

You now have a good idea of what happens during bankruptcy and the steps for becoming eligible for it. However, before you file you might want to consider the implications of filing for bankruptcy, specifically how this will affect your property.

One of the first things to consider is equity. Throughout this book, the term is used to refer to any type of property in which there is some value in a mortgaged property that is more than that owed under the loan. For example, if you have a mortgage on your home for which you owe $120,000 and that home would be worth $200,000 if it was sold today, you have about $80,000 worth of equity. Equity is important in bankruptcy because it is an asset you own. In some situations, you may have to sell your property if you have plenty of equity in it and use the sale profits to repay your lenders.

The second term you need to learn about bankruptcy and your property is **bankruptcy estate**. This simply refers to any real property you own during the time of your bankruptcy case, which is subject to that bankruptcy case's rulings. "Real property" is anything tangible, including cash, real estate, and personal property. However, defining what that property is and how it is affected by your bankruptcy is more challenging. At the time of filing for bankruptcy, everything that you own comes under the authority of the bankruptcy court to determine what to do with it. There are exclusions to this rule, but for the most part, you do not lose ownership; however, you may lose control over what happens with the property at the time you file. The bankruptcy estate is comprised of any type of property that is under the bankruptcy court's jurisdiction.

There are several ways to break down this property to get a good understanding of what is in control of the bankruptcy court and what is not. However, each state also has specific rules in place. The information listed here refers specifically to federal laws regarding property, but your state's laws may be slightly different. Your attorney will help you with state laws, or you can find this information on your state bankruptcy court's Web site.

The property you own and possess: One of the first distinctions made is in regards to ownership and possession property. This includes any type of property you may have in your home, such as your television, clothing, computers, tools, real estate, stock certificates, or even artwork. This is all included in your bankruptcy estate. Any property that belongs to another person is not part of your bankruptcy estate. This includes any property that you may control but do not own. Specifically, if you do not have the right to sell or give away that property, it cannot be part of your bankruptcy estate. If you do not own it, creditors cannot seize it.

The property you own, but do not possess: On the other side of this issue is property you may own, but that you do not have direct control over. However, any property that you own is part of your bankruptcy estate, even if physical possession of the property is not in your direct control. This may include things like vacation timeshares, deposits in the control of a stockbroker, or even royalties and commissions for something you own, such as the royalties from a book or a sale. Even the security deposit you have is considered to be your property and, therefore, may be part of your bankruptcy case.

Did You Just Give Property Away?

One of the mistakes many people make when it comes to filing for bankruptcy is trying to give property away to someone else in the hopes of protecting it from the bankruptcy courts. In fact, it used to be somewhat common for some attorneys to tell bankruptcy filers to do just this to protect the property from the courts.

However, this is a mistake to avoid. It is easy to consider giving your property to friends and relatives or to pay preferred creditors before you file. However, there is no benefit in doing this. Any property that you have given away or paid out in an anticipation of filing for bankruptcy is still part of your bankruptcy estate. The trustee of the court may take this property back from wherever it has been placed if the trustee learns of it. How will the trustee know? When you sign your bankruptcy documents, you must report all property transactions that have occurred over the last two years. If you sign this document without listing something that has taken place, you are perjuring yourself, and failing to report a transaction is a felony. If the transfer of property did occur and you did not report it, the trustee will seize the item and sell it to pay your creditors back for it. More so, there is likely to be prosecution of the perjury charge. That may cause the bankruptcy court to refuse to hear your case.

The other mistake many people make is to pay off a preferred creditor prior to filing for bankruptcy in the hopes of keeping the account open and active. You may like the rewards offered by one creditor, for example, and therefore want to keep that line of credit open. Doing this could backfire, too. One of the elements of bankruptcy is all creditors are to receive treatment equally. This includes family members, businesses, credit card companies, and medical billing companies. In many instances, creditors do not get anything under bankruptcy. If you pay one of your unsecured creditors, you are being unfair to the other creditors.

One specific consideration is the rule of insiders, who are your family, friends, and business associates. You cannot make a payment of more than $600 to any specific creditor from this group in the year prior to filing for bankruptcy. Perhaps you borrowed some money from a parent for an emergency, and when your tax refund came, you paid them back. If it was more than $600, you are in violation. This means, the trustee can strip back that money and use it as part of your bankruptcy compensation to creditors. Further, your case may be thrown out for such actions. In the court's opinion, if you can make a large payment like this to a family member, you should have paid it back to your lender. You may not have any idea you plan to file for bankruptcy in a year.

Nevertheless, such money can be taken back from the person you paid it to by the court to repay your loans instead, or they may require you to refund this money to the creditor.

There are a few specific exemptions here. For example, if you are making a payment to someone who is not an insider, who is anyone but a relative, friend, or business associate, the court may not have a problem. Rather than looking back over a period of a full year, the court only looks at transactions back three months in the case of non-insider creditors, which accounts for most individual's creditors. Furthermore, if most of your debt comes from your business activities, the court will look at all transactions that took place over the last year, but the limitation of what it will act on is currently set at $5,475 per transaction in terms of what your business has paid out. For example, if your business has paid a business contractor $6,000 for services, the court may want to know what that payment was specifically for to ensure it was not a way to skirt repaying lenders.

Property You Are Entitled to Later

Any type of property you are entitled to receive, but have not received, is still considered part of your bankruptcy estate. This includes all types of wages that you have earned, but have not yet been paid or any tax refunds legally owed to you. There are many types of property this could entail, including:

- Property you are entitled to receive from a trust, including periodic payments you receive from the trust. The entire trust is part of your bankruptcy estate and should be included, even though the trustee may not be able to get funds from it.

- Any vacation time or severance pay you have earned before you filed for bankruptcy may be included.

- Any type of property you have inherited (typically from someone who has died) but have not received at the time of filing for bankruptcy.

- The proceeds from an insurance policy may also be part of your bankruptcy estate, including payments you received as a beneficiary on a life insurance policy.

- A legal claim to monetary compensation is part of your bankruptcy estate, even if the value of that claim has yet to be determined: for example, winning a lawsuit where you are entitled to monetary compensation. Any accounts receivable that you are owed are considered part of your bankruptcy estate, even if you do not believe you will be paid for them.

- Any money earned by any property that is within your bankruptcy estate is also included in that estate, including rent from a property you own or royalties from the copyrights you own.

There are also certain types of property that may be included in your bankruptcy estate if you earn or obtain them within 180 days of filing your bankruptcy case. This includes property that you inherit during the 180-day period. It also includes property you may obtain from a property settlement agreement or from a divorce decree that goes into effect within this period of time. This does not include alimony, though. In addition, if you receive death benefits or life insurance policy proceeds that become owed to you during that 180-day period, those too become part of your bankruptcy estate. Because you do not have these to report at the time of filing your bankruptcy claim, you will need to include a supplemental form after you have filed bankruptcy.

Marital Property

In some situations, filing for bankruptcy jointly makes sense, especially when both people accumulate the debt and it is in both names. It is up to you to determine if you will file separately or jointly. You may not want to file bankruptcy alongside your spouse in many situations, though. If most of the debt is in one person's name, for example, you can protect the credit score of the other by allowing only one person to file. The decision to file jointly or to file alone needs to be one you make based on the circumstances. Consider what exactly your marital property is before you make a decision about which way to file.

The property that you and your spouse own together is included in your bankruptcy estate, depending on if you file jointly or alone and the laws within your state. If you do file jointly, then all property that fits into any of the previously described categories will be included in your bankruptcy estate, regardless of who legally owns it. If you want to keep property separate and out of bankruptcy, avoid filing jointly. However, it is a different situation if you do not file for bankruptcy jointly. If you are married but file for bankruptcy alone, some of the marital property may not be considered part of the bankruptcy estate and may be left off your bankruptcy documents. This could protect it from creditors and help you to avoid losing some assets. This depends on where you live, because property laws are based on state laws. In the United States, there are several types of marital property states: community property, tenancy by the entirety, or common law states. These differences determine how property is organized for ownership.

Community property states

In community property states, any property that is earned or received during the marriage is considered "community property" and is therefore owned by both parties. There are some exemptions, such as gifts and inheritances received by only one spouse. In addition, any property owned prior to the marriage or that is received after permanent separation of the marriage is not included as community property.

If you live in one of these states, are married, and are filing for bankruptcy alone, then any property you or your spouse own — community property — is included in your bankruptcy estate. This is true even if one of you does not file for bankruptcy. Any property that is considered separate, such as gifts, inheritances, or properties obtained before or after the marriage, is not listed in the bankruptcy estate.

The following states are community property states:

- Alaska (In Alaska, this is only true if the spouse signs a written agreement to treat the property as community property)
- Arizona
- California
- Idaho

- Kansas
- Louisiana
- Maryland
- Nevada
- New Mexico
- North Dakota
- Texas
- Washington
- Wisconsin

Tenancy by the entirety states

In "tenancy by the entirety" states, any type of real estate (and in some states, any type of personal property) owned by the couple belongs to the marriage itself, rather than to one spouse or the other. If you file for bankruptcy together, all of this property is added to the bankruptcy estate. In cases where only one spouse files bankruptcy, the property is not part of the bankruptcy estate and it may be exempt from the claims for which only one of the spouses is liable. The reason for this is simple: The property belongs to the marriage, which means that one spouse does not have sole control to give it away or sell it. One spouse may not encumber that property with debts either. If there are debts which both spouses take on together, this property is then included in the bankruptcy estate.

The following are tenancy by the entirety states:

- Alaska
- Arkansas
- Delaware
- District of Columbia

- Florida
- Hawaii
- Maryland
- Massachusetts
- Michigan
- Mississippi
- Missouri
- New Hampshire
- New York
- New Jersey
- North Carolina
- Pennsylvania
- Rhode Island
- Tennessee
- Vermont
- Virginia
- Wyoming

Common law property states

In all other states not listed thus far, **common law marital property** applies. In this case, when only one of the spouses files for bankruptcy, all of the spouses' separate property, plus half of the couple's jointly owned property, will be part of the bankruptcy estate. In other words, any property you own outright is part of the bankruptcy estate, and half of what you own with your spouse is also included in the bankruptcy.

What is separate property, then? Any property that has only one spouse's name on the title is that person's sole property. This includes titles for vehicles, houses, stocks, or other property with an official title. In addition, if the property was purchased, received as a gift, or inherited by you and your spouse, then both of you won the property and half of it would be subjected to the bankruptcy estate. Any property that one spouse purchases with his or her personal, separate funds is that person's sole property. However, there must be proof that this is the case in the form of documentation, such as a title or receipts showing how the property was purchased.

Common law property states include:

- Alabama
- Colorado
- Connecticut
- Georgia
- Illinois
- Indiana
- Iowa
- Kansas
- Kentucky
- Maine
- Minnesota
- Montana
- Nebraska
- Ohio
- Oklahoma
- Oregon
- South Carolina
- South Dakota
- Utah
- West Virginia

What constitutes marriage?

Today, the laws for defining marriage are ever changing. Same-sex couples and domestic partner laws differ from state to state. In short, legalized same sex-marriages are new to the system, and neither the process nor the precedence for how bankruptcy affects these couples is known. This includes any situation in which you are registered legally as partners or married under the state's laws. In situations where you do have legal standing as a married couple, then the rules of married couples would apply. The state defines what is considered a married couple or a legally registered partner. However, if the state has yet to define these laws, you may or may not be able to file for bankruptcy jointly.

The biggest obstacle you will face is federal law. For example, federal laws do not, as of yet, recognize same-sex marriages or domestic partners; therefore, the legal proceedings for bankruptcy, which occur in federal courts, may not allow these couples to file for bankruptcy together. Also, keep in mind that property ownership for those who own property together, but are not registered as a domestic partnership or a same-sex couple, does not change. In other words, if you have not registered, then laws regarding bankruptcy filing for just one person are no different from filing for bankruptcy if you were outside of this union. Any property that you own, whether shared or not, is included as part of your bankruptcy estate. It is always best to consider an attorney for these complex rules.

Property that is Not Part of Your Bankruptcy Estate

So far, the rules on types of property that are included in your bankruptcy estate have been discussed, but there are also some types of property not included. This property is not subject to the bankruptcy court's jurisdiction, meaning that the bankruptcy court or the trustee is unable to take this type of property from you, sell it, and use the proceeds to pay off your creditors. The following are just some of the types of property that may not be included in the bankruptcy estate, but this might not be an exhaustive list for your state:

- Most property you buy or you receive after the date that you file for bankruptcy.

- Property that is in your possession, but belongs to someone else, including property you are physically storing at your residence.

- Property that is pledged collateral for a loan, if the licensed lender retains the possession of the collateral (such as a pawnbroker).

- Any type of pensions and retirement plan funds.

- All tax-deferred education funds.

- Wages that are withheld, including employer contributions that are made for the employee benefit and health insurance plans.

- Funds placed in a qualified tuition programs are protected from the bankruptcy estate as long as you deposit these funds into these accounts at least a full year prior to filing for bankruptcy and they are for a child, stepchild, foster child, or grandchild.

Property you can keep

Under bankruptcy law, the term property refers to everything that you own. If you own your home or you have ownership interest in land or buildings of any type, you own real property. For those who do not own any type of real estate, everything else that you own is personal property.

In Chapter 13 bankruptcy, the goal is to keep all of your assets, which will happen as long as you work through the repayment plan thoroughly. You will not have your property subjected to sale, because you are still working to repay those funds. However, if you do want to let some of this property go, and therefore forgo repaying it as part of your bankruptcy plan, you can do so, but the funds received due to the sale of the property will be used to repay the debt with the creditor.

On the other hand, when you file Chapter 7 bankruptcy, you may be able to keep some of your property, depending on the type of property and your state's specific laws. In many cases, you may be able to keep your home. However, other types of real estate in which you have equity will be sold to benefit the creditors holding loans against those properties, such as a rental property or a second home. If you have real property owned outright, the sale of that real estate is likely to repay your creditors.

In most cases, you will also be able to keep most of your personal property. This will depend on if it is exempt under your state's exemption system. Understanding exemptions is important, as it can help you determine if you should file for bankruptcy. However, the topic is not an easy one to comprehend outright.

Exemptions

Property you are legally able to keep during and after bankruptcy is **exempt property**. Finding out what you are legally able to keep when filing for bankruptcy is not the easiest process, but it is something you need to do. The easiest way to learn which exemptions you can take is to speak with your bankruptcy attorney, who will have the most updated information available for you for the state where you are filing for bankruptcy. However, it is your responsibility to claim all of the exemptions you are entitled to when you file for bankruptcy. If you fail to take an exemption, you could lose that property to the bankruptcy estate and then to creditors unnecessarily, and there is no reason to allow this to happen.

Exempt property may include your home, clothing, and retirement account. The more property listed as exempt, the better off you will be when filing for bankruptcy. Remember, when filing Chapter 13, you are not likely to lose any of your property unless you decide to let it go. However, in Chapter 7 bankruptcy, you could lose anything not listed as excluded from the bankruptcy estate.

The exemptions you are allowed to take are based on your state's legislature and the rules it has set forth. You must be a legal resident of that state to take advantage of that state's exemption laws. However, there are also federal exemptions. In 15 states, you are able to choose either your state's exemptions or federal exemptions (which are created by Congress). These include:

- Arkansas
- Connecticut
- Hawaii
- Massachusetts
- Michigan
- Minnesota
- New Hampshire
- New Jersey
- New Mexico
- Pennsylvania
- Rhode Island
- Texas
- Vermont
- Washington
- Wisconsin

Federal exemptions are determined by Congress in bankruptcy code and include the following:

- Real property is protected up to $20,200, which includes including mobile homes and co-ops; up to $10,125 may be used for other types of property. **Real property** is any physical property, such as real estate.

- Vehicle is protected up to $3,225 in value.

- Animals, clothing, furnishings, household goods, musical instruments, and crops are protected for up to $525 per each item in value and up to $10,775 in total value.

- Jewelry valued up to $1,350 is protected.

- Up to $1,075 in any type of property is protected, as is any unused portion of the homestead exemption up to $10,125.

- Health aids are protected fully.

- Lost earning payments are protected fully.

- Personal injury recovery funds up to $20,200 are protected, except for any payments made as pain-and-suffering payments or payments made from pecuniary loss.

- Wrongful death recovery payments are protected if the person who died is someone you depended on.

- Public benefits including Social Security, unemployment compensation, public assistance, and veteran's benefits are protected fully.

- Compensation from any type of crime you are a victim of are protected fully.

- Pensions, including retirement accounts, IRA, and Roth IRA accounts, are protected up to a value of $1,095,000 per person.

- Alimony and child support payments are fully protected.

- Tools of the trade, including books, implements, and tools used in your business are protected up to $2,025.

- Insurance is protected fully for unmatured life insurance policies except for credit insurance, life insurance policies with a loan are protected up to a value of $10,775, and insurance from disability, unemployment and illness benefits are protected fully. Life insurance payments that come from a person you depend on for support are fully protected.

Exemptions differ from state to state. For example, in the state of Arizona, the homestead exemption is valued at $150,000. In Alaska, the homestead exemption is $67,500. The federal homestead exemption is $20,200 (listed above as real property).

In some states, you must choose one set of exemptions (either state or federal), but you cannot choose which individual exemptions to take. For example, you cannot pick the federal homestead exemption and then choose a state exemption for your vehicle. You can amend this decision later after filing your bankruptcy paperwork if you would like to, for example, if you find that you may benefit under the other option more so. Use Schedule C (one of the bankruptcy forms) to do so.

In the state of California, a unique exemption system is in place. The state does not allow debtors to choose the federal exemptions, but it does have two sets of state exemptions from which you can choose. The alternative California exemptions are the same as the federal exemptions with a few minor differences. Visit California's bankruptcy court Web site to learn more, or ask your attorney which set of exemptions are better for you. In all other states, you are required to use the state's specific exemptions for filing for bankruptcy.

There are several types of specific exemptions you should be aware of when preparing to file for bankruptcy. These are most important to consider. The first is a **limited amount exemption**, which protects the value of your ownership in a particular item, but only up to a limit. For example, some state exemptions allow you to keep up to $4,000 worth of equity in a vehicle, which is the value that is no longer under a loan. This means that as long as the equity in your car is under $4,000, the car is exempt from the bankruptcy estate. If the car's equity is above that $4,000 mark, the vehicle may be subject to sale by the trustee. It is important to note, in this type of exemption, the only way you will be able to keep such property is to remain up to date on payments. If you fall behind or are significantly behind at the time of your filing, chances are good that you will lose the property to the bankruptcy estate.

Another type of exemption is a "**without regard to value exemption.**" As the name implies, these are specific types of property that are exempt from the bankruptcy estate no matter what the value is. This may include things like your refrigerator, your microwave, or carpeting. Any property that is considered an exemption without regard to value will be listed specifically on your state's bankruptcy laws as being such.

There are also **wildcard exemptions**. This particular type of exemption gives the bankruptcy filer a dollar amount that may be applied to any type of property he or she owns. If you own property that is not exempt under any other exemption, and the value of that property is under the state's wildcard dollar amount value, you can keep it exempt by applying that value to your property. For example, if you own a motor home valued at $4,000 and that motor home is not exempt under any of the state's exemptions but the state has a $5,000 wildcard exemption, you can apply the value of the motor home under the wildcard exemption to protect it from the bankruptcy estate. You can also use a wildcard exemption to increase the exemption to a limited amount. If your state offers a limit of $4,000 on a vehicle's equity, and it offers a $4,000 wildcard exemption, your vehicle valued at $6,000 may receive protection from the bankruptcy estate.

Why is there so much difference from one state to the next? Ultimately, the laws of the state are defined by the state's legislature, which is influenced by the attitudes of the people living within the state. Because each state has the right to set limits as it sees fit, there are all sorts of differences in these exemptions. Because they are so different, it is important for you to consider your state's specific exemptions, as defined by the U.S. courts in your state. To find your state's exemptions, visit your local bankruptcy court's Web site or office.

Have you just moved?

Under the old bankruptcy laws prior to 2005, individuals could move to another state, wait a few months, and then file for bankruptcy in that state. Some might have done this to take advantage of better exemptions in one state compared to the next. In an effort to reduce the number of people who would do this, the new bankruptcy laws put in place domicile requirements for using state exemptions. Your domicile is defined as the place you live. It is where you are a registered voter, where you get your mail, and where you pay taxes. Even if you are living in another place temporarily, your domicile is defined based on these other factors. The new laws regarding bankruptcy set the limits on where you can file for bankruptcy. If you have made your domicile in the state you are currently living in for the last two years, then you will use that state's exemptions. If you have lived at your current state for more than 91 days but less than two years, you must use the state's exemptions for the location you lived in for the better part of the 180 days immediately prior to the two-year period preceding your filing. If, however, you have your domicile in your current state for less than 91 days, you can either file in the state where you lived immediately before or you can wait until you have hit 91 days and then file in your current state. You must have lived in the previous state for 91 days or more in order to use that state's exemptions.

For example, this might occur when you move from one state to the next for a new job. For example, if you move to Ohio in June from Michigan and want to file for bankruptcy in August in Ohio, you would need to use Michigan's exemptions. If you file for bankruptcy in October, you still would use Michigan's exemptions because most of the two years you lived in Michigan.

In those situations where the state you are filing in offers a choice between the federal exemptions and the state exemptions, you can elect to use the federal exemptions no matter how long you have lived in that state. Federal exemptions are not specific to where you live. In addition to this, it is important to note that homestead exemptions have a longer domicile requirement than those listed thus far. If you purchased your home within 40 months before you filed for bankruptcy, your homestead exemptions will be subject to a cap of $136,875, even if the state's homestead exemptions available to you are larger. *More information on homestead exemptions can be found in Chapter 1.*

It is important for you to think about your situation carefully before you file if you have recently moved. If waiting a bit longer may help you to qualify for better exemptions, it is often best to do so. On the other hand, if filing sooner means a larger exemption option, do so faster.

Married and filing jointly are different

Most married people will do better to file for bankruptcy jointly. Just like filing your taxes, you have the ability to choose when and how you will file for bankruptcy (jointly or alone). If all of your debt is in one person's name, it might be best to file for bankruptcy without your spouse, as this protects your spouse's credit, and some of your jointly owned assets may receive protection depending on the where you live.

However, most married couples will file for bankruptcy jointly because it can help to get more of the debt included, and it can allow for larger exemptions. If you are married, are filing jointly for bankruptcy, and the federal exemptions are available in the state where you file and you decide to use them, you may double all of your exemptions. This is possible because both you and your spouse can claim these exemptions each to the full amount allowed under the federal exemption. However, you can only use one exemption system: if your spouse uses the state's exemptions, you cannot use federal exemptions.

If you are married and filing jointly and decide to use state exemptions, then you may be able to double them. This is dependent on the laws of that state. In some cases, only some of the exemptions may be doubled or not all. For example, in California in its first system of exemptions, the exemption for motor vehicles may not be doubled; however, the exemption for tools of the trade may be doubled in some circumstances. The ownership of the property is also important. In order for you to receive double exemptions on a piece of property, it must be jointly owned. If there is a title that gives ownership of the property to someone, it must have both names on it for you to receive double exemptions on that property.

To make matters a bit more complicated, this area of bankruptcy law is one that changes often in some states. It is always in your best interest to speak with your bankruptcy attorney about your options and specifically about your exemption choices as well as how they affect your case before you file. Exemptions themselves can be one of the most lucrative ways to save money and property when filing for bankruptcy, so it is important to consider all of your options.

What Do You Own?

Now that you have an idea about what exemptions are, you might be looking around trying to determine what property you own that may be at risk of being lost or that may fit under these exemptions.

When you file for bankruptcy, you will be required to list all of the property that you own that belongs in your bankruptcy case. (Your attorney will help you through this process if you have one.) However, it is your sole responsibility to make sure that everything you own is included in a thorough inventory, especially when filing Chapter 7 bankruptcy, to ensure that the debt is discharged if possible. Whether you can keep this property depends on what the property is worth and what your state's exemptions are. The best way to know where you stand is to take a complete inventory of your belongings. What should you include? List everything worth value in your home and in the bank. Here is a quick look at some of those items:

- All cash, including what you have in your home, your wallet, and even that hidden stash

- All of the deposits of money you have, including bank accounts, brokerage accounts, certificates of deposit, credit unions, escrow accounts, money market accounts, savings and loan deposits, and even the money you have in a safety deposit box

- Security deposits, including those for your gas, electric, heating oil, rental unit deposits, upfront paid rent, and telephone

- Household goods, including any antiques, appliances, dishes, food, electronics, yard equipment, furniture, video equipment, and outdoor furniture

- Print material in your home, including valuable pictures, books, and art objects (including stamps, coins, and other collections)

- Clothing, furs, and leathers

- Jewelry, including watches and rings

- Sports equipment, firearms, and hobby equipment

- Insurance policies

- Annuities

- Profit sharing plans and pensions, retirement accounts, stocks, bonds, interests in partnerships, and government or corporate bonds

- Accounts receivable from a business or commissions that you have already earned

- Alimony or child support payments or other payments that you receive due to divorce or childcare

- Any other debts you may have outstanding that are owed to you, such as disability benefits, workers compensation, wages due, Social Security benefits, and judgments that you have won

- Interest in other property that you have due to another person's death

Not all of this is subject to actual bankruptcy estate; however, it will be important to list it all. It is better to list items as part of your household inventory which you know are not going to be subject to bankruptcy estate, then it is to omit them and be accused of trying to hide something of value. Now, it is also important to point out that your creditors will not have access to your home, and your trustee is unlikely to pay a visit to your home (though they can). You should be thorough, but if you forget to mention one pot or pan, you should not have a problem.

What should you do with the information that you have just created? Create a list of each of the items you own. Sometimes, the best way to do so is to use a video camera and walk around your home. Write down each of the items that you own on a separate line on a piece of paper as you watch the video. You will need to include the following for each item:

- Provide a brief description of the item.

- Provide the property's replacement value — this is not the price you paid at the time of purchase, but the cost of buying a replacement of the item right now. This is likely to be more expensive than what you paid originally.

- List the exemption that the property applies to or what you believe it applies to.

- List the number of the statute where that exemption appears. You will be able to fill this in when you are filling out your bankruptcy paperwork, because that is where you will find the specific exemption numbers listed.

Your goal here is to determine what you own and then to determine if there are any exemptions that will protect your property from the bankruptcy court. Follow the next steps to do so.

1. Once you have made this list, determine if there are any pieces of property you plan to let go. For example, if you owe $5,000 on a vehicle you no longer want to own, do not worry about finding an exemption to cover that; you will be able to forfeit the vehicle in bankruptcy.

2. Next, determine if a state exemption will cover your property. If your state exemptions do not cover enough of the property or cover the property at all, note this. Then, look to see if your state has a wildcard exemption in place. Later, you can determine if you can place the property under the wildcard exemption.

3. Next, consider the federal exemptions, if you live in a state that allows for it. If you live in California, check the second set of exemptions within the state. If you find that

your property fairs better under these federal exemptions, it may be best to file for bankruptcy using them. However, you do want to take the time to compare the state and the federal exemption options you have (if you have the ability to use either choice). Be sure to look for a federal exemption wildcard that can also help you.

4. If you have the choice, decide which of the exemption options is right for you. Do this by looking at what is covered under each type of exemption and then factor in the overall difference. Remember: You may qualify for double exemptions if you are filing jointly and factor that into the equation too.

In addition to this, note any property you may lose during the bankruptcy case. Unfortunately, unless you can save your property as exemption property, it is likely that you will lose the property during bankruptcy. As with all other aspects of filing for bankruptcy, talk with your attorney before you make an ultimate decision regarding exemptions. As long as you trust your attorney, chances are good he or she will be able to help you to make the decision on which type of exemptions are best suited for your needs.

Selling nonexempt property prior to filing

If you have significant nonexempt property, it may be tempting to try and sell it to purchase exempt property or to simply get the funds liquidated from the property. However, you need to be careful when doing this and it is often not advisable to do so.

If the trustee learns you are in fact selling property that is nonexempt in an effort to avoid paying creditors with those funds, this may amount to fraud. If the trustee believes you sold the property to hinder, shortchange a creditor, or to otherwise hide the funds or property so your creditor cannot take it, your bankruptcy may be thrown out. Furthermore, if you buy exempt property using money from your sale of nonexempt property, the court can treat the new exempt property as nonexempt.

If you need to sell the property, or you feel you should be able to do so, speak with your attorney about doing so before you actually make this decision. In some cases, it may be completely allowable for the process to occur, such as the examples below. The following are some examples of how you can turn nonexempt property into exempt property, though your state's laws may be different.

One way to do this is to replace any nonexempt property you may have with exempt property. This includes selling the property that is nonexempt and using the money from the sale to purchase exempt property. An example here might to be sell your valuable jewelry to purchase clothing for your children, which is exempt in most states.

Another route is to purchase property that is exempt up to a certain value, without going over that value. If you have a sizable amount of cash in your checking account, which is not usually exempt, you may wish to purchase a new computer for your business with the funds to avoid the loss of the cash. Some people might choose to sell their nonexempt property and use the proceeds from that sale to pay down debts. If this is something that you are considering, remember that there are rules about paying down debts just before your bankruptcy. You should not pay off a debt ahead of time that could be discharged in bankruptcy, because most of these debts will be completely discharged. One option to consider is paying off a small credit card if you wish to keep that credit line available to you after your bankruptcy. If you do not owe anything to the lender, it does not need to be filed into the bankruptcy and can remain open.

You should not pay more than $600 toward any of your debts or to anyone that you owe money. If you do this, you could place that payment at risk, because there are limits on how much of a payment you can make to a single creditor prior to your bankruptcy. In addition, if you use these proceeds to pay down secured debts, such as your car loan or your home loan, you could find that doing so pushes the value of these items too high against what is allowable as exempt property. For example, if you owe $1,500 on your car loan for your second vehicle and you sell an expensive coin collection for $1,500, you may be tempted to pay off that car loan with the funds. The problem here is that you are over the $600 limit, and the bankruptcy court may take the car to pay down your creditors. On the other hand, if you kept the car loan in place and kept making your monthly payment as normal, that asset might still be yours after bankruptcy. Finally, you can and should keep making your monthly payments in their regular amounts. This includes all of your utility costs and your mortgage or rent. Even if these payments are normally more than $600 per month, you still need to pay them and they do not count against you when you file for bankruptcy.

Keep it in the clear

As you work towards bankruptcy, you will need to make various decisions. You will need to make decisions about which lenders to file and which ones not to. You may have to make some critical decisions about property that you own, even property that is sentimental to you.

As you do so, be sure to follow these preplanning guidelines. You want to avoid any type of problem that could arise due to a decision you have to make before filing for bankruptcy.

- **Your home's equity**: If you apply a homestead exemption to cover your home's equity, this is fine. However, if you try to convert nonexempt property, the amount of your homestead exemption could be reduced dollar for dollar over that nonexempt property. Before you attempt to do this, contact your lawyer to find out how your local bankruptcy court handles this type of situation, because this is often done on a case-by-case basis.

- **Be thorough and accurate**: When it comes to your financial transactions, leave a paper trial. In fact, use the Statement of Financial Affairs form, Form 7 of your bankruptcy paperwork, to complete these details. If the trustee questions why you made any of these decisions regarding your nonexempt property, simply tell the court that you were trying to give yourself a better start after bankruptcy. The trustee is more likely to agree with you in this situation than to throw out your case.

- **Keep it even**: If you sell a piece of art worth $400 and you buy work tools valued at $400, this is rarely a problem. On the other hand, if you only spend $200 on those work tools, this will be a problem with the trustee. Show where the transaction occurred and make sure it is an even trade of nonexempt property for exempt property. Also, be sure to keep these transactions at market value. Selling your $500 television to your friend for $50 will cause a problem.

- **Do not wait**: Do not wait until the month before you file for bankruptcy to make such changes in your property. This looks suspicious. The longer the time between when you file for bankruptcy and when these transactions occur, the better. If you wait until the week before you file to sell your nonexempt valuables, this is clearly intended to cheat creditors.

- **Avoid changing only ownership**: The money needs to change hands, not just the actual ownership of the item. A good example of this occurs when only one spouse files for bankruptcy. When the filing spouse changes ownership of a rental property he owns in his name only to his wife, for example, this is clearly an instance where the individual wants to defraud creditors.

Why does all of this matter so much? When you look at the picture in a different light, you can see why judges and trustees are concerned about how you are moving your property around. Hypothetically, say you took out a credit card agreeing to pay back the money you borrow. Then, you used that credit card to buy a new television. Then, when you could not repay your credit card, you took the television you bought using the creditor's money and sold it to someone else. Clearly, this is dishonest behavior. Keep in mind that you need to show your creditors you are not trying to deceive them by being honest about such transactions in your bankruptcy paperwork; show that you are making wise decisions for your financial future under the letter of the law.

Your Home and Bankruptcy

Your home might or might not survive bankruptcy. If considering Chapter 7 bankruptcy, you need to know that the bankruptcy itself will not protect your home. Chapter 7 bankruptcy does lead to an automatic stay, which freezes your lenders from collecting debt or taking secured debt from you. This automatic stay is only in place while your bankruptcy case is pending, not after it has been discharged.

For the average homeowner, there are two significant risks that need to be taken into consideration here. First, if you are behind in your mortgage payments, Chapter 7 bankruptcy will not stop foreclosure from occurring. You will need to continue making all of your payments to the lender before, during, and after the bankruptcy. If you are currently behind on your mortgage payment, you will need to get caught up in your payment if you plan to keep your home. Chapter 7 bankruptcy does not encourage, nor ensure, that lenders will restructure your loan for you. Second, if you have nonexempt equity in your home — any type of equity you have that is not exempt by your homestead exemptions or other exemptions — your home could be used to repay creditors in Chapter 7 bankruptcy. However, this is not likely to happen if you are caught up on payments and the amount of equity in your home is less than enough to cover the costs of selling the home.

On the other hand, those filing Chapter 13 bankruptcy will get a break when it comes to saving their home. Like other debts you have, the Chapter 13 restructuring plan will help you to get your home mortgage back on track, if you are in fact behind on your payments. Most people will be able to remain in their homes because lenders will want to work with you if you are in Chapter 13 to ensure they are able to get their money back. Further, in this form of bankruptcy, the goal is not necessarily to sell off your assets to repay your creditors. Rather, it is the process of restructuring your debts so that you can pay them off. With Chapter 13, you have the ability to keep your assets as long as you plan to repay them; secured assets like your home will be paid in full.

Bankruptcy and a foreclosure

A typical homeowner going through bankruptcy can expect a few things to occur. No matter what form of bankruptcy you are filing, you will need to keep making your mortgage payment. If you stop making your mortgage payment in Chapter 7 bankruptcy, the lender is likely to pursue your case through foreclosure. Essentially, if you want to remain in your home, make your payments.

If you have any type of lien on your home, such as a tax lien, your bankruptcy is unlikely to reduce or discharge these liens. A second mortgage, home equity loan, or home equity line of credit is also unlikely to be discharged. Any time you use your home as collateral against a loan, it is unlikely that you will be able to get out of paying those funds back without losing your home in the process. This is the case because these are secured loans, backed by the collateral you placed on the loan. The only type of lien that may be forgiven during Chapter 7 bankruptcy is a judgment lien, which is a particular type of lien placed on your home from a creditor. If a creditor has taken you to court for nonpayment, the judge may rule that you must either pay your debt or you will be unable to sell your home without paying that debt. This is known as a **judgment lien**.

What if you are behind on your home loan but you want to stay in your home and file Chapter 7 bankruptcy? Filing for bankruptcy itself will not fix the problem, but that does not mean your lender will not work with you. As soon as you find yourself unable to make a payment on your home loan, contact your lender. If you are filing Chapter 7 bankruptcy, inform the lender that once your other debts are discharged (such as your credit card debt and personal loans) you will have the monthly payment to stay current on your mortgage. Ensure the lender knows you have the means to repay your debt. Request that missed payments be added on to the end of your mortgage loan, as well as a restructuring of your mortgage.

Your lender can work with you several ways by:

- Allowing you to continue make payments while tacking on any missed payments to the end of the loan.

- Dividing up the amount of money you are behind over a period of several months to make it easier for you to repay.

- Allowing you to make an interest-only payment.

- Allowing you to sell your home to repay your debt, which can help to save your credit score from the added difficulties of foreclosure.

- Restructuring or refinancing the entire loan in the hopes of reducing what you owe in back payments and allowing you to get into a lower monthly payment, if it is possible to do so.

If you find yourself in a situation where there is no way for you to get out of a foreclosure that is pending, talk with your bankruptcy attorney about your options. He or she may offer to represent you when discussing these options with lenders. If the foreclosure is likely to go through, choose the type of solution that is best suited for you, based on the options you have. The first solution may be to simply sell your home. When you sell your home, you avoid foreclosure, which is damaging to your credit report. Further, by avoiding foreclosure you will have an easier time getting into another home loan in the short term. If you are like many who have seen a significant drop in the value of their home and you cannot sell the home for a high enough value to cover the mortgage loan, ask your lender to work with you by agreeing to a short sale. In a short sale, the lender agrees to accept less than what is owed on the home loan. This scenario has become more common as the number of home value drops have risen.

You could try to refinance the loan, too. If you want to remain in the home, contact other lenders and request a new loan. A new loan will pay off the first loan and give you a fresh start. This may not be an option if your credit is very poor or you have not shown that you are able to make repayments on the loan.

For those who are older than 62, another option is a "reverse mortgage." This type of mortgage allows the lender to take legal claim to the home, and in turn pay you a monthly, quarterly, or lump sum payment. However, until the death of both you and your spouse, you can remain in your home. At that time, your lender allows heirs to purchase the home, if they would like to, or sells the home.

If these solutions do not work and you want to remain in your home, the best option is to file Chapter 13 bankruptcy instead of filing Chapter 7. This requires that the lender work with you to restructure the loan to make it easier for you to pay. You can also use Chapter 13 to help you to get rid of any liens on your home.

Too much equity

Another problem you may face when it comes to your home and bankruptcy is equity, which is the amount of unmortgaged value of a home. In other words, if you know what your home is worth and subtract any type of loan or lien on your home, the remaining value is equity. If your home is worth $500,000 and you owe $300,000 on it, you have $200,000 worth of equity. Not all homeowners have equity, particularly if their home value has dropped or they have just started repaying their loan.

As discussed earlier, you are allowed certain exemptions in regards to your home's value. Your homestead exemption will likely include the equity in your home, up to the value based on the type of exemptions you take (state or federal) and the laws of the federal government or your state. The trustee is looking at your home's value in another way. The goal of Chapter 7 bankruptcy is to repay creditors with any assets possible, outside of the exemptions. In other words, if they took your home from you and sold it, would there be anything left to repay your creditors? If so, is that value higher than what the allowable exemptions are? If so, then the trustee may determine that your home should be sold to repay your debts. To determine this yourself, follow the following steps:

Get an estimated value of your home. You may wish to have your home appraised, but this could cost several hundred dollars. There are house-valuing tools available from real estate agents as well as on the Web you can use. Zillow (**www.zillow.com**) is an excellent choice, for example. This estimate is not necessarily how much you owe on the home or how much you purchased it for.

Determine the cost of the sale. This includes paying for closing costs and real estate agents. The trustee is likely to figure the cost of selling the home at between 6 to 8 percent. Determine what 8 percent of your home's value is.

Add up what is owed on your home. This includes the mortgage you currently have plus any liens against your home. This includes any secondary mortgages, tax liens, and other liens.

Take the total from the first step and subtract the totals from the second and third step. If you have a positive number here, this is the amount of equity in your home, and it is subject to being liquidated if it is above your exemptions.

For example, assume your home is worth $300,000, the cost of sale is $20,000, and you still owe $290,000 on the mortgage loan. Because $300,000 minus $20,000 minus $290,000 is a negative number, there is nothing to repay creditors with. However, if you only owed $200,000 on that home, there would be $80,000 left to repay creditors and therefore the home might be sold.

Is your property exempt? This depends on several factors, including the type of exemptions you are using. If you have moved from one state to the next, before you take your state exemption, consider the following. If you purchased your home less than 40 months ago, you can use your current state's exemptions. If you bought your home at least 2 years ago but bought it within the last 40 months, the maximum exemption you can take is $136,875, unless you purchased your home using the funds from the sale of another home within the same state. If you purchased your home less than two years ago, you must use the exemptions of the state where you used to live. You also have an exemption limit of $136,875, according to state and federal exemptions.

In those states where you are able to choose between the federal and the state exemptions, you should always choose the federal exemptions, because they allow you to protect up to $21,000 worth of equity in your home. Married couples can double that equity value. Unless your state's homestead exemption is higher than this, use the federal exemptions.

Therefore, to further the math process above, compare what exemption you are using against the current value of equity in your home. If the value is still a positive number, you likely have too much equity, which may require you to sell your home to repay your lenders.

Let us look at another example: James and Jenna have a home valued at $180,000. They hope to file Chapter 7 bankruptcy but want to remain in their home. They owe their mortgage lender $144,000 on their home, but they also have a home equity line of credit for another $12,000. This means they have $24,000 worth of equity in their home ($180,000 minus $144,000 minus $12,000). They live in a state that allows for federal exemptions, so they decide to use those for their homestead exemptions. This means that $42,000 worth of equity is allowed in their home for them to keep the home. Therefore, they are likely to be protected as long as they stay current on their monthly mortgage payments to keep their loan agreement with their lender in good standing. The federal exemption thus protects their property.

Three states do not have homestead exemptions:

- Maryland
- New Jersey
- Pennsylvania

In the District of Columbia, there is an unlimited homestead exemption. If you live there, you do not have to worry about losing your home to creditors in Chapter 7 bankruptcy, because your home is totally protected regardless of the amount of equity you have in the home. Some states have a homestead exemption based on the lot size of your home. This includes the following states:

- Arkansas
- Florida
- Iowa
- Kansas

- Oklahoma
- South Dakota
- Texas

In these states, the amount of your homestead exemption is based on how large your lot is. You can find these specific numbers in your state's listing of exemptions. In these states, if your home's lot size is lower than the exemption allows, then your home is completely protected from your creditors. If it is larger, you will need to determine if federal exemptions are available and if so, if your equity is under that value.

In some states, the homestead exemption is based on both the size of your lot and equity in your home. This includes the following states:

- Alabama
- Hawaii
- Louisiana
- Michigan
- Minnesota
- Mississippi
- Nebraska
- Oregon

If you live here, the trustee will look at your lot size first. If your lot size is higher than what is allowable, the trustee will want to sell your home. If your lot size is smaller than the exempted level, the trustee will then focus on your equity. If it is under the required level, then this means your home is protected from creditors.

Other states base the amount of your homestead exemption on equity alone. That includes the following states:

- Alaska
- Arizona
- California
- Colorado
- Connecticut
- Georgia
- Idaho
- Illinois
- Indiana
- Kentucky
- Maine
- Massachusetts
- Missouri
- Montana
- Nevada
- New Hampshire
- New Mexico
- New York
- North Carolina
- North Dakota
- Ohio
- Rhode Island
- South Carolina
- Tennessee
- Utah
- Vermont
- Virginia
- Washington

- West Virginia
- Wisconsin
- Wyoming

In addition, all federal exemptions are based on equity only. If you live in one of these states, determine what the state's homestead exemption is. If your home's equity is higher than this amount, then it is likely that it will be sold to allow creditors to be repaid.

Preventing home loss

For those who do have equity that is valued higher than what is allowed, there may be a way to reduce that equity under the state or federal limits so you can remain in your home. The following options might allow you to avoid foreclosure, but keep in mind that it is always best to speak with your attorney first to ensure you are not violating any of your state's laws regarding bankruptcy exemptions.

In some cases, you can use your nonexempt equity to pay off other debts to help you to avoid bankruptcy, too. If you have enough equity in your home, you may want to consider doing this. For example, if you have $10,000 in equity that is not exempt, you may wish to pull out this money and use it to pay off another loan. However, keep in mind that you are using secured loans to pay off unsecured debt, which means that you are going to have to repay your debt in full if you plan to keep your home.

There are two main ways to save your home by reducing your equity. You can do this by borrowing against your equity, or you can sell partial ownership of your home. Before you consider either one, consult your attorney. If you do decide to borrow against your equity, such as securing a home equity loan from a lender, you will not be reducing the amount of the debt you own, only trading in high interest rate debt like credit cards for lower interest rate, secured debt. For example, if you take out a home equity loan for $10,000 and you pay off several credit card lenders with this money, you are trading that high interest rate debt (the credit cards) for a lower interest rate secured loan. However, your home is now on the line for repaying that debt.

Those who are looking to proceed like this should be careful in terms of who they pay and how much they pay to each lender, because the trustee will monitor any payments more than $600 to any one person or lender. In addition, those who are in financial turmoil may still qualify for a secured loan, but the interest rate and closing costs of such a loan will be significantly higher because you are more of a credit risk.

The other method to reducing your equity is to sell a portion of your home's ownership to someone else. A formal title change and sales contract needs to be made through a title agency to do this. This way, you do not have to be worried about making another monthly payment as you would if you obtained a loan on your equity. You might have a friend or family member who is willing to purchase a portion of your home, such as a share in it. If you go this route, it is likely you will need to wait two years to file for bankruptcy. The trustee is likely to see this as a way of defrauding creditors, especially if you sold the portion of your home at a bargain price to your friend or family member. For example, if you sell a part ownership of your home to your brother, the property is no longer equity. However, if you sell at a low price, below what is considered its value, this could be considered defrauding.

Again, if you want to avoid having to lose your home, often the best method to do so is to file Chapter 13 bankruptcy rather than Chapter 7 as you will not lose your home in this method. Rather, your debt is reorganized and repaid.

Your Secured Debts

Your mortgage is a form of secured debt, but there are other types too. Just like your mortgage, some type of security backs these debts. The lenders on these loans have a right to be paid in full or they may repossess the asset from you. Further, if these assets are valued high enough with too much equity, the trustee may wish to strip them from you and sell them to repay your creditors. There are some levels of security in place; however, you have to consider each type of security you have carefully. There are numerous types of secured debts, and each of these needs to be dealt with. Other than mortgages and home equity loans, determine if you have any of the following types of secured debts:

- **Loans on cars**: The car is the collateral on the loan, and the lender will repossess it if you default on the loan.

- **Loans on boats, motorcycles, RVs, tractors, and other types of equipment and vehicles**: The vehicle is collateral, and the lender will repossess it if you default on the loan.

- **Store charges**: Some types of store charge accounts are backed by collateral. Most stores no longer have secured charge accounts, but there are some that will hold any of the merchandise you charge to the credit card as collateral on the loan. If you fail to make payment, they can repossess it.

- **Secured personal loans**: These may come from banks, credit unions, or other finance companies. Often, you will place some type of asset as collateral on the loan, which may be your valuable personal property, like a paid-off vehicle or expensive jewelry. If you default on the loan, the lender can take possession of anything you used to secure the loan.

Some types of secured debts are exempt under state laws, such as your first car loan, assuming you are current on the debt. In other words, if you owe money on a vehicle and keep making on-time payments, then the lender is unlikely to repossess the debt, and the trustee will mark it as exempt property. If you have any of these types of debts, you may want to find a solution prior to filing for bankruptcy for dealing with the debt. The first thing you can do is simply to surrender the asset to the lender.

For example, if you have a second car loan that is nonexempt property under the exemptions you are taking, rather than holding on to the vehicle, you give it back to the lender. However, it is possible you can still be liable for any value in that loan, which is unpaid by the value of the collateral. For example, you own a vehicle worth $3,000, but your loan still has a balance of $5,000. You decide to give back the car to the lender to get out of the debt. There is a balance of $2,000, which you are liable to repay. This is an unsecured debt, which is likely to be discharged during bankruptcy.

Another option is to avoid or eliminate **liens**, which are any holds against your property made by a creditor. This is a legal procedure in which you ask the bankruptcy court to actually avoid liens on your exempt property. To avoid or eliminate this type of debt is possible under certain circumstances. The value of the property and the amount of the exemption determine whether you can use this method to protect your property. If the property is worth less than the exemption limit, the court will eliminate the debt in total. In this situation, you keep the property without having to repay any of the debt in Chapter 7 bankruptcy. If the property is worth more than the exemption limit, the bankruptcy court will reduce the lien by as much as the exemption is worth. Take this example: You owe $2,000 on a piece of property that is exempt up to $1,600. In this situation, the courts will require that you owe $400 on that property at this point, ($2,000 minus the $1,600 exemption). In either of these situations, you keep the property and have the debt either eliminated or reduced significantly.

Another way to deal with your secured debts is to reaffirm the debt, which means to tell the creditor you want to keep paying the debt as it stands. You might want to do this if you want to keep the property and keep the loan. When you do this, both the creditor's lien on the property and your personal liability to that debt will remain after you file for bankruptcy. You will not lose the property during bankruptcy and the lender will still have the right to collect payment from you after the bankruptcy for the full value of the lien. In most cases where you are up to date on your loan, the creditor will send you correspondence once they are notified of your bankruptcy through the trustee. Although larger creditors will do this automatically, if there is a smaller creditor that does not, you can contact the lender directly and ask to reaffirm the debt with them. Most will be happy to accept as long as you are making payments on the loan.

When you reaffirm your debt with a lender, you do commit to repaying the loan. If you default on the loan before, during, or after the bankruptcy, the lender has the right to repossess the property from you.

In any of these situations, your attorney can help you with the process of protecting your property in bankruptcy. Be sure to consider all debts you have that are secured. Then, determine if you want to keep the assets or you want to allow the lender to take it back. Work with your attorney to protect any assets possible, especially nonexempt property. However, keep in mind that not all property can be kept. Your creditors have the legal right to any nonexempt property, and the trustee will want to liquidate anything possible to repay your creditors.

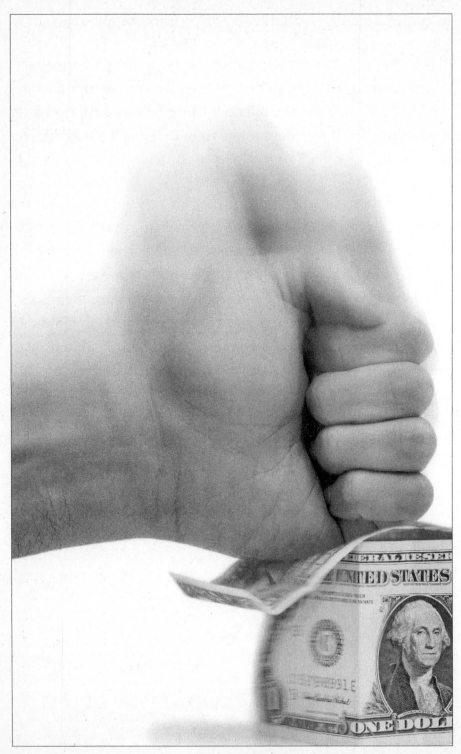

CHAPTER 5

COMPLETING CONSUMER BANKRUPTCY

Throughout this book, information has been provided in an effort to help you understand the bankruptcy process, including what the consumer bankruptcy outcome is likely to be for you. You understand now what bankruptcy is, what exemptions are, and how to protect your property. The information in this chapter outlines what you need to do to actually file for bankruptcy, including the procedure for filing. However, keep in mind it is best to work with your attorney through the bankruptcy process. An attorney can guide you through the process easily and ensure that any type of exemptions you qualify for are obtained. If you have special circumstances, such as excessive nonexempt property or secured debts, it is critical to use an attorney to protect as much of your property as possible.

Nonetheless, even if you do use an attorney, it is important to know what is happening in terms of filing for consumer bankruptcy. There are numerous forms and a great deal of information you need to supply to the trustee in the case, to ensure that your bankruptcy case is successful. There are several pieces of information you need to gather before you even begin filling out your bankruptcy paperwork. *To find out more about hiring a bankruptcy attorney, look back in Chapter 2.*

Documents Necessary to File

As mentioned throughout this text, the new bankruptcy laws enacted in 2005 have made filing for bankruptcy more difficult. These laws aim to keep people from filing for bankruptcy if there is any way they can avoid it. One of these new complications is that you now need to supply the bankruptcy court with a significant amount of documentation, whereas the old laws allowed you to simply give your word.

You will need to provide a certificate that shows you have completed the necessary credit-counseling workshop. You also need to provide all of your wage stubs and income reports for the last 60 days. You will need to provide your most recent tax return.

Counseling certificate

The credit counseling workshop certificate is a document that shows you have completed a workshop within the last 180 days prior to filing for bankruptcy. Every person who wants to file for consumer bankruptcy must attend consumer credit counseling. A U.S. trustee must approve of this organization. You can find a list of approved organizations at the United States Department of Justice Web site (**www.justice.gov/ust/eo/bapcpa/ccde/cc_approved.htm**). This counseling may be completed over the Internet, in person, or even over the phone. Once this process is completed, the organization will provide you with a certificate of completion. This certificate will need to be attached to your bankruptcy petition when you submit it.

The point of this type of counseling is to find out if you can enter into a repayment plan to pay off the debt that you owe. Attorneys will often encourage those who are filing for Chapter 7 bankruptcy to avoid the repayment plan if they feel they will be unable to sustain the payments easily.

You do need to go to a counseling session to get your competition certificate. Once you file for bankruptcy, the trustee will look at the actual repayment plan the counseling agency worked out. If the trustee believes you have the ability to work through a repayment plan, the trustee might not be willing to allow you to have your debt discharged, but instead may require that you complete a Chapter 13 bankruptcy to repay some of your debts.

Tax returns

In addition to the counseling certificate, you will need to submit your most recent tax forms with your bankruptcy paperwork, but this form can be submitted as late as seven days before the meeting with the creditors. Your creditors may also request a copy of your tax return. If they do request it, you are required by law to provide it. Your local IRS office can supply a copy of your most recent tax documents. The IRS will give you a transcript that includes basic information from your tax return. This transcript can be a substitute for your actual tax return when you file your bankruptcy paperwork.

Wage stubs

You need to provide the bankruptcy court with a record of how much money you have made, too. You need to show the trustee what amount of money you have made in the last 60 days. The easiest way to do this is to submit official wage stubs from your employer. If you do not have 60 days worth of wage stubs, ask your employer to provide you with a copy of them. For those who are not employed and have no income, there is no requirement for you to file these wage stubs; your bankruptcy paperwork will show that you do not currently have any income.

Paperwork Requirements

Filing for bankruptcy is something you need to do with your local bankruptcy court. Therefore, the paperwork and the exact details will be specific to your area. Each court has its own specific requirements, such as filing at specific offices or filing a state form for administrative use. If you fail to meet these specific guidelines, your case could be thrown out of court. To find out your local rules, determine where your local bankruptcy court is. You can do this by visiting the U.S. Courts Web site (**www.uscourts. gov/courtlinks**). In some cases, you will need to visit the court to obtain the necessary paperwork, especially in larger cities where there simply is not enough manpower to answer your questions over the phone. Otherwise, many of the bankruptcy courts have their own sites where some or all of the paper work can be downloaded or can be requested. If you are working with an attorney, your attorney will handle obtaining all of the paperwork for you.

Some forms are standardized and are used in all bankruptcy cases. Some local courts will have specialized forms, such as unique ways to report wages, or they may require some additional information. The other thing to remember about local paperwork requirements is that every detail matters, from the way that you sign the date to the order you file the papers. If you make a mistake, the trustee can send it all back or just reject the case. When you visit your court, look for a sample form and application so you are aware of the correct order.

Required forms and documents

The Federal Office of the Courts provides very specific and official forms that have to be completed to file for bankruptcy. These forms are standardized throughout the bankruptcy courts, but as mentioned, local courts have additional forms you will need to file. Once you have the necessary preliminary documents — your wage stubs, tax forms, and your counseling certificate — you can begin working through the actual bankruptcy documents. You will then need to attach any and all local forms as required by your local bankruptcy court. If the local bankruptcy court requires you to file these papers in a different order than what is listed here, do so.

Most of these forms require basic information stated in fill-in-the-blank style format. You should be able to work through most of them easily. Most forms require minimal math computation with the rest requiring straightforward information, such as names of creditors and debt amounts. The tedious process of filing out multiple forms should be fairly painless, if you have taken the time to work through all of the information included in this book, up to this point. You will know what the questions about exemptions mean, for example.

If you come to a form listed here that does not apply to you, you must still file that form to ensure all documentation is provided as required. However, there will likely be a box on the top portion of the form that will allow you to make note that this form does not apply to you. The most common instance of this occurring is with real estate. If you do not have real estate, simply check the box stating you do not, include the form in your packet, and then continue with the subsequent forms. While filling out the required paperwork, keep the following questions in mind:

- **Did you make several copies of the forms?** You will want to make copies of the forms after you fill them out for your own records, but before you get started, copy the forms. This way, if you make a mistake, you have backup forms.

- **Did you type the final forms to turn in?** It is often best to employ a typewriter (your local library should have one) to fill in these forms. You cannot fill these out online, and unless you have some type of software program to aid you, your computer will not work either. Your attorney will do this for you if he or she will be submitting the information. Though you can print them and turn them in, this only increases the risk that you will have to be contacted for clarification.

- **Where you completely thorough?** Give too much information rather than not giving enough information. This is rather important because you want to ensure that you are providing everything that could be needed. If the paperwork must be sent back to you for corrections, there are chances that it could be thrown out.

- **Did you check to ensure each question has been answered?** If you are unsure of how to fill something out, ask an attorney. Whatever you do, avoid leaving anything blank, as this will delay the process for you. Anything not filled in means you did not fill the form out thoroughly.

- **Did you use a second paper if you ran out of room?** Although most of the time there is plenty of space for you to fill out the forms, if there are situations where you need more room, take a blank piece of typing paper, label it with your name, the form name, and the question you are further answering; then submit that, in order where it belongs, with your bankruptcy paperwork. This is common practice.

- **Did you sign the documents?** You — and your spouse, if he or she is filing with you — need to sign the bankruptcy petition and have each of the pages dated as it requests. Be sure the date matches on all pages of the petition. Jointly filed applications require only one application with both of your information listed on them.

- **Did you follow directions for putting the forms in order and punching holes in them if required?** Most of the time, you will need to put the forms in order and then use a two-hole punch in them. Do not staple them together, as this is the required procedure. Follow all directions provided in the forms that are supplied to you.

- **Did you include your filing fee?** This may be paid in a money order made out to the bankruptcy court. Submit this payment by clipping it to the petition. Most bankruptcy courts will not accept a payment in cash or check.

- **Did you submit them directly to the correct bankruptcy court?** You should turn in these forms in person rather than in the mail. It provides you with the best possible result, because it ensures that your paperwork has gotten to where it needs to be according to schedule.

Once you have done all of this, take a deep breath, but realize things are going to change. Every aspect of your real property and your financial life will be affected in some way by the filing of this bankruptcy petition, from your spending habits to what you own.

The first thing that you will notice is, the minute you file for your bankruptcy, the automatic stay goes into effect. That means, above everything else, you can get the creditors to stop calling you. If they do call, especially within the first few weeks, simply alert them to the fact you have filed bankruptcy as of the date you filed and the creditors will stop calling. It is legally necessary to supply this information at least one time if a creditor contacts you.

The second most important thing to know about the moment after filing is that, legally, all of your bankruptcy estate is now in the control of the trustee. Technically, you no longer own your property at this point in the process as the bankruptcy trustee is in legal control over it. However, it is unlikely that the trustee will actually take physical ownership of your property, especially because most filers will not lose their property through bankruptcy. For example, the trustee can decide to sell property if he or she determines the equity should repay lenders. Once your bankruptcy case is discharged, the ownership of your property comes back to you, unless it was sold to repay creditors as mentioned above in regards to equity.

Checklist for Chapter 7 bankruptcy

The following is a list of all of the federal forms you need to file with your bankruptcy court. You can get these forms directly from your local bankruptcy office. This extensive list ensures you have submitted all required forms according to federal guidelines, though your state or local bankruptcy office may require more forms to be filed.

☐ Form 1: Voluntary Petition

☐ Form 3A: Use this form only if you want to pay the required filing fee in installment payments.

☐ Form 3B: Use only if you are applying for waiver of the fee due to special circumstances.

☐ Form 6: Multiple parts, including each of the following:

o   Schedule A: Real Property Form

o   Schedule B: Personal Property Form

o   Schedule C: Property Claimed as Exempt

o   Schedule D: Creditors Holding Secured Claims

o   Schedule E: Creditors Holding Unsecured Claims (Priority Claims) o   Schedule F: Creditors Holding Unsecured Claims (Non Priority Claims)

o   Schedule G: Executory Contracts and Unexpired Leases

o   Schedule H: Co-Debtors

o   Schedule I: Current Income

o   Schedule J: Current Expenditures

o   Summary Form for Schedules A through Schedules J

o   Statistical Summary of Certain Liabilities

o   Declaration Concerning Debtor's Schedules

☐   Form 7: Statement of Financial Affairs Outlined

☐   Form 8: Chapter 7 Individual Debtor's Statement of Intentions

☐   Form 21: Full Social Security Number Disclosure Form

☐   Form 22A: Statement of Current Monthly Income and Means Test Calculation

☐   Form 23: Certification of Instructional Course on Financial Management

☐   Form 201: Notice to Individual Consumer Debtor Under § 342 of the Bankruptcy Code

☐   Mailing Matrix

Checklist for Chapter 13 bankruptcy

The following is a list of all of the documents you need to submit if you are filing Chapter 13 bankruptcy.

☐ Form 1: Voluntary Petition

☐ Form 3A: Use this form only if you want to pay the required filing fee in installment payments.

☐ Form 6: Multiple parts, including each of the following:

o Schedule A: Real Property Form

o Schedule B: Personal Property Form

o Schedule C: Property Claimed as Exempt

o Schedule D: Creditors Holding Secured Claims

o Schedule E: Creditors Holding Unsecured Claims (Priority Claims)

o Schedule F: Creditors Holding Unsecured Claims (Non Priority Claims)

o Schedule G: Executory Contracts and Unexpired Leases

o Schedule H: Co-Debtors

o Schedule I: Current Income

o Schedule J: Current Expenditures

o Summary Form for Schedules A through Schedules J

o Declaration Concerning Debtor's Schedules

☐ Form 7: Statement of Financial Affairs Outlined

☐ Form 21: Full Social Security Number Disclosure Form

☐ Form 22C: Chapter 13 Statement of Current Monthly Income and Calculation of Commitment Period and Disposable Income

- ☐ Form 201: Notice to Individual Consumer Debtor Under § (section) 342 of the Bankruptcy Code

- ☐ Mailing Matrix

- ☐ Chapter 13 Repayment Plan

What Happens After You File Chapter 7

In the next few weeks, the bankruptcy trustee will process your bankruptcy petition. As for you, there is little you will need to do, unless there is some type of clarification that is needed regarding your forms; this will be requested by the trustee through a formal letter or phone call.

You can go back to day-to-day living, but you do need to be mindful of your spending habits. You do not want to use credit cards at this point. You should keep submitting payments on those loans you plan to repay, and you should stay within a budget and not attempt to take on any new credit. You should not make any significant purchases, especially those more than $600, but you should pay your bills as you have been for assets you plan to keep, such as your home loan and your utilities. Keep in mind that you should also use this time to determine how you can avoid getting back into this position again, such as making and sticking with a budget and living within your means. Choose a cash-only budget, which means you can only buy what you have the cash on hand to buy.

The process starts when the bankruptcy court sends a notice of bankruptcy filing to each of your creditors. On your **mailing ma-**

trix, a form within your bankruptcy paperwork, you will list each of the creditors you wish to be addressed during the bankruptcy process. This notice is sent to each of those.

Your creditors will receive the filing date and the case number. This notice to the creditor also tells the creditors about your assets so they can see what you own and the likelihood that a complaint would be worth their time. If you do not own any property that is not exempt, they may not be able to get any money from you and therefore they may not bother to come after you. Specifically, it states whether the case is an **asset case** or a **no asset case**. When you were filling out your bankruptcy papers, you had to state whether you believed there were any assets or funds available for distribution to the creditors, or if there were no expected funds available after exemptions and administrative fees were paid. This information is sent to the creditor, though the court can change this later if it determines that you do, in fact, have assets that can be used to repay some or all of your debts.

The notice also notifies you of your creditors' meeting. The meeting of creditors, or **341 meeting**, will occur several weeks after this notice is sent. You will receive notice of this date as well, and you need to pay attention to it, because you are required to attend this meeting. If you fail to make this meeting, your case may be discharged. Your creditors have 60 days following this meeting to file any claims against your assets, if your case is an asset case. As for your role in the creditor meeting, you will simply give your name and answer questions about why you are filing for bankruptcy. Very limited communication with you is necessary, as this meeting is a formality to allow creditors to bring complaints against you and for you to enter the legal proceedings of bankruptcy. If no creditors bring complaints within those 60 days, your case moves forward to discharge.

Any type of objection creditors have also must be filed at this time. In the objection, the creditor is attempting to have the court review the terms of the lender's agreement in the hopes of having the court order you to repay the debt. This can happen, but it is unlikely.

The notice also provides information to the creditor in regards to your trustee, including his or her name and contact information. Generally, you will not have any reason to contact your trustee during this time, and you should avoid calling to inquire about your case. It is critical to keep the trustee looking positively on your bankruptcy to avoid any type of negative results. You want the trustee not to have a negative viewpoint of you. Bothering one about your case will not bode well with a busy trustee.

After you file, your phone should stop ringing. Once the creditors receive this official form, the automatic stay has gone into effect and creditors have to stop all collection activity against you, at least until the bankruptcy case is settled. After your bankruptcy case has been settled, the court will alert the creditors, letting the individual companies know the result and whether the creditor has the right to pursue your case and further.

There are several exemptions to the automatic stay, including:

- Any criminal case you may be a part of can proceed against you. The automatic stay has nothing to do with any legal battles you are facing in a criminal court of law.

- Some types of evictions can go forward, especially those that have nothing to do with your finances.

- Tax-related audits, issuances of tax deficiency notices, and demands for payments from the IRS are exemptions.

- Any legal case that is establishing paternity, to collect or modify child support or other cases having to do with alimony or child support payments are an exception to the automatic stay.

Keep in mind: The first time your creditors call you after you have filed your bankruptcy, the company is unlikely to know about the bankruptcy filing, unless you have notified the creditor previously. Be polite and inform the caller that you have recently filed for bankruptcy. Also provide any information you have, such as your case number, trustee information, or the date you filed. The creditors receive a letter in the mail about the same time that you do. Prior to that, you will need to inform them of your bankruptcy filing.

Further, if the creditor has received information about the bankruptcy and the financial company continues contacting you, then it will be in violation of the automatic stay. Report this directly to the bankruptcy court and to your trustee. In some situations, it may be worth contacting your lawyer, too, because this violation could allow the debt to be reduced or eliminated. However, the process is complex and does require an attorney to determine if you have a case or if you should just dismiss it and move on.

The meeting of creditors

If the name of this meeting sounds daunting, it is because the event can seem quite intimidating until you walk in, sit down, and answer a few questions. In most bankruptcy cases, this is all that needs to be done at this meeting. However, it can be a bit more complex, depending on the rules of the bankruptcy court you are in and the details of your case in general.

At the creditors' meeting, also called the 341 meeting, your trustee will be present rather than a judge. Remember: This person is not necessarily working for you (that is what your lawyer is for), but the trustee is representing the court. Therefore, be polite and be sure to remember the trustee's opinion does matter. The trustee will ask you many questions, which he or she might have regarding the paperwork you turned in prior to this occurrence.

There is no way to know what questions the trustee is going to ask. Each case is unique. The trustee has the authority to question every line of your bankruptcy paperwork if he or she would like to, though most do not. The trustee will ask about anything that seems out of the ordinary or leads him or her to believe you are hiding something from the court or are trying to take advantage of your creditors. Various examples of questions are provided later in this chapter.

In some cases, the trustee will ask to see documentation of information you have included in your bankruptcy petition. For example, the trustee may ask for documentation that shows the value of your home. Plan ahead by bringing any information pertaining to your case with you, especially when it could be something the trustee questions. However, if the trustee should ask for some type of documentation and you do not have it, the trustee is likely to stop the meeting and reschedule it. Inquire about this with your attorney, and he or she will help you determine the necessary documentation that you should bring with you for your meeting of creditors. In some cases, documents can be submitted through the mail, after the creditors' meeting. There are a few things you will definitely want to bring to the meeting, including:

- Documentation that shows how much your income is at the time of the creditor meeting, especially if the wage stubs you submitted with your bankruptcy petition do not show an accurate representation of what you are making right at the time of the legal gathering.

- Copies of your current statements from your financial institutions. You also want to show any statements from your investment accounts.

- Documentation or proof of your current budget, outlining your expenses and income.

- Photo identification.

For those who are not using an attorney, take the time a few days prior to the meeting of the creditors to call the trustee directly and request information on any documentation that should be brought with you. Contacting him or her prior to the meeting of creditors is not a problem, but avoid calling after this meeting occurs. In most cases, the trustee will have your details available to provide this information to you, but do not be alarmed if he or she cannot. In some bankruptcy courts, there are simply too many cases for the trustee to handle to be able to take phone calls regarding each one. Take the documentation listed above and plan to submit anything additionally requested at the meeting afterwards, though this could delay the meeting if the information is needed.

The good news is, for most bankruptcy filers the meeting of the creditors will take less than 15 minutes and is simple. You will arrive and have to wait your turn among other filers. Once your name is called, you will likely have a private meeting with your attorney and the trustee present, which is audibly recorded as any legal proceeding is. The trustee will ask you to take an oath that you will tell the truth throughout the meeting, and then he or she will ask general questions, such as why you are filing, what caused your financial distress, and if the information you have provided is accurate.

However, if you fail to attend this meeting, the trustee may automatically schedule your case to be dismissed, without discharging your debts. There is simply no way around attending this meeting. If you know there is a conflict, contact the trustee in advance to try to reschedule, but you will need a very good reason to back up your need to reschedule. Most trustees will reschedule the meeting one time for those who have a valid reason, such as a verifiable medical excuse or an immediate family emergency.

You will be sworn in during the meeting of the creditors. If you make false statements here, or regarding your bankruptcy petition, you could be found in contempt of court. Be honest. Be sure that all of your documentation is completely honest and accurate, too. One aspect to remember about this meeting is, the trustee will look you in the eye and ask if all information is accurate. If he or she believes in any way that you are lying to the court, the trustee will likely give a more thorough questioning process regarding your bankruptcy petition to verify each detail.

The biggest holdup for most people is that they are concerned about the questions that the trustee may ask. There is no way to know for sure what will be inquired until you arrive at your meeting and the questions begin. However, there are a few standard questions listed below. Know the answers to any and all of these that pertain to your individual bankruptcy case:

- Did you sign and submit the petition for bankruptcy, including each of the schedules, statements, and other documents that are contained within this packet? (Here, the creditor is verifying that you are presenting this information as factual).

- Do you understand all aspects of the paperwork you have submitted, including what all of the figures on these forms are and what they mean?

- Is the information contained in these documents accurate, to the best of your knowledge? Has anything changed since you have filed these documents that makes the information within them inaccurate in any way?

- Have you listed all of your assets thoroughly on the proper schedules? Have you left out any assets intentionally or unintentionally?

- Have you listed all of your creditors on the schedules provided?

- Have you filed for bankruptcy in the past? (If the answer here is yes, be prepared to present the discharge date and the case number of your previous bankruptcy filing for verification to ensure you are able to file for bankruptcy again.)

- Do you own real estate? Do you have any financial interest in any real estate? If yes, what is the value of that real estate compared to what you owe through mortgages and liens?

- How did you determine the value of any of the real estate that you have included here?

- If you are renting at your current address, have you owned real estate in the past? If so, is the current owner of the real estate someone who is related to you?

- Have you transferred any type of real property in the last six months? If so, why and what was the value of that property?

- Have you made any payments to any creditor, friend, or family member in the last six months that was higher than $600? If so, why and what was the amount?

- Is anyone holding any property you own or that you will receive in the next year?

- How many vehicles do you own? Do you have loans on those vehicles and if so, what is the value of these assets?

- Do you have any winnings from a lottery or other gift to declare?

- Are you listed as a beneficiary on any life insurance policies, settlement documents, or other investments?

- Have you been involved in any business in the last year? If so, what is that business? Is the business still operational? What is the value of the assets of the business?

Once the trustee begins to go through the documents you have submitted, he or she will ask you questions about specific items. If your answers are different from what is listed on the forms, this indicates some dishonesty to the trustee. This is why it is important to go through your paperwork before your meeting to know what the details are.

After the trustee's questions have been answered, your creditors who have come to the meeting are able to speak. In most cases, no creditors come to the meeting, because most cases are not asset-based cases and they are unlikely able to collect on the debt. Financial institutions are only likely to send a representative to the meeting if the creditor believes it can gain something from you, such as liquidating assets they know you own. Most creditors in attendance are secured creditors, who do not necessarily want to liquidate assets, but instead want to verify your intentions of repaying the debt you owe.

Another instance when creditors may come to the meeting is if there has been major use of their credit cards or sizable loans taken out just prior to filing for bankruptcy. The creditor will question what the money was used for to determine if its services are being abused. Once the creditors are done questioning you, the meeting is over.

In a busy bankruptcy court, the entire meeting of creditors is likely to last less than five minutes. Even in other courtrooms, ten minutes is usually the top end of how long this meeting could take. Unless there is a dispute between you and one of your creditors, such as the ability to discharge a debt because of wording in a contract, you will be able to leave. If there is a dispute, then you will need to allow the court to rule on this, which may take some additional time, even as long as a month. In most cases, this is not necessary.

Once the meeting of creditors is over, this starts the 60-day waiting period. During this time, creditors have the ability to file a claim against any assets you own, or dispute the bankruptcy in any way. This normally does not happen, unless you have nonexempt assets. Once the 60 days is up, the bankruptcy case moves forward.

If you are filing Chapter 13, the process is very similar to what is included above. The only difference is, there is a period of three to five years where you will be paying off your debt. This period of time occurs prior to the scheduling of the meeting of the creditors. In short, you will file your bankruptcy paperwork just as you did above. Once the trustee verifies the plan and approves it, you enter the repayment phase. That phase will take between three and five years to complete, as determined by your individual case. The meeting of creditors only occurs after the debts have been repaid. This meeting is then for those creditors whose debts were discharged. Under most Chapter 13 plans, some unsecured debt is discharged. Those creditors have the right to come forward now before that discharge formally occurs.

After you have worked through your repayment plan, any debt that will be discharged will then be presented to the court through the formal bankruptcy petition, as it is for Chapter 7 bankruptcy.

Debtor education course

There is one final step before your debt will be discharged. As part of the law changes made in 2005, a debtor education course was added to the requirements of the bankruptcy process. This debtor education course occurs after your meeting of the creditors. You should complete it as soon as possible to prevent any hold on your bankruptcy discharge from occurring.

The debtor education course is a two-hour long financial management course. The course must be obtained from an approved agency. You are often able to take this course through the same agency that you worked with to get your credit counseling prior to filing for bankruptcy. You can also find a list of approved organizations providing this course by visiting the U.S. Department of Justice (**www.justice.gov/ust/eo/bapcpa/ccde/de_approved. htm**).

This course will cost between $50 to $100 to complete. You are able to take this course online, by telephone, or in person through the arrangements you make directly with the agency providing the course. The course will is designed to provide helpful tips and resources to help better plan your financial future, so that you do not end up in financial turmoil again. The course goes over budgeting, saving, and the use of credit and loans.

Once you have completed the two-hour course, you will be given confirmation numbers or other completion documentation. You will need to submit this, along with Form 23 of the bankruptcy paperwork, to the bankruptcy court. Do this no later than 45 days after your meeting of the creditors. If you fail to turn this form in on time, your entire case can be thrown out because of it.

Cases of nonexempt property

In some cases, there will be nonexempt property that needs to be relinquished from you and given to the trustee, who will then handle the sale or trade-in of the item. For example, if you have a second home, the trustee will take official ownership at the time of your filing the bankruptcy petition and later turn ownership over to the lender who has secured the debt. You will know this is occurring because it is likely part of the reorganization plan.

At your meeting of the creditors, the trustee will collect any non-exempt property, or property that is not protected by an exemption. Generally, the trustee will allow the exemptions you listed on your bankruptcy paperwork, assuming they fall under the appropriate federal or state exemptions. Any nonexempt property is to be sold by the trustee in order to produce money for the creditors to put towards your debt. At this point, the goal of the trustee is to simply collect as much money as possible from your bankruptcy estate that is nonexempt, to turn it into money for your creditors.

At this point, you may have enough money to pay for some of your property. If you were supposed to lose a piece of art as non-exempt property, you can trade cash for the property at your meeting of creditors. However, you will need to state where the funds come from. You may have come into some money, or you may have borrowed funds from a family member to make the trade. However, it is the trustee's decision whether or not you are able to trade cash for the item. Each case is unique, and there is no way to know if the trustee will allow it. You should only plan to do this with nonexempt property you absolutely cannot separate from, because you will have to pay the replacement value of the item, which is the amount it would cost to buy the item today. Something that cost $200 ten years ago may cost $400 today to replace, for example.

In addition, the trustee is likely to allow you to trade nonexempt property for exempt property. If you want to keep your art collection, but would rather trade in your car for it, the trustee will likely allow you to do this, assuming the value is equal or more than the nonexempt property. The goal of the trustee is to get every penny he or she can for your creditors. Any nonexempt property needs to be turned over to your trustee or to the creditor at this time. Titles will need to change hands using a title agency. Any tangible property needs to be provided to the trustee according to the trustee's instructions. You will no longer be able to use that property.

The Discharge Hearing

Most people will not have to attend a discharge hearing. Most courts no longer schedule discharge hearings because the process is a formality and, in busy bankruptcy courts, it is difficult to have enough time to hold such a hearing. **Discharge** is used to describe the action in which the bankruptcy is completed and the debts you have requested to be relieved of are no longer required to be paid by you. If you are required to attend a discharge hearing, which is rare and at the trustee's discretion, you will be notified of this hearing about 45 days after your meeting with the creditors. The meeting involves you and the bankruptcy court judge. The judge looks over your case and will explain what happens if the debt is discharged, such as the effects on your debts. The judge determines if your debts are paid appropriately or if you should still be held responsible for something not as of yet repaid. The judge often has a stern discussion with the filer to ensure he or she understands the importance of what has occurred during bankruptcy. The judge wants to be sure you are not planning to file for bankruptcy again, and that you will have learned your lesson from this occurrence.

Once the discharge hearing is complete, you can leave the court. It is likely that you will receive your discharge documents within four weeks after this meeting. Your debt is not officially discharged until you receive official documentation from the courts saying so.

Now the waiting begins. Generally, you will wait up to three months to hear back from the bankruptcy court. A notification will come to you in the mail outlining the discharge of your debt. This official notice is all that you need to know your debt has been discharged and you are no longer responsible for it. It will state that the bankruptcy court has reviewed your case and that all debts listed within your bankruptcy petition have been discharged.

The discharge order is an official form that comes from the bankruptcy court. The front of the discharge order provides some basic information identifying the case. Flip it over and you will learn if your debts have been discharged. If so, the document will state this. If some or all of your debts have not been discharged, the document will outline this information in categories.

There are many reasons why your case may not be discharged. These include any of the reasons listed thus far, such as:

- Failure to take a means test.
- A creditor disputes your case and the trustee believes the dispute is valid.
- Missing filing deadlines.
- Suspicion of abuse of the bankruptcy system.

The discharge notice is incredibly important. You will need it throughout the next few years to show proof of your debt being discharged, such as a collection company trying to make a claim against the debt. Make several copies of this paper and keep it secure.

Making changes after receiving a discharge notice

You have your bankruptcy discharge in hand, but then you realize that you still have other debt — debt that should have been included in the bankruptcy. It is sometimes the case that you can forget a lender or overlook a specific debt. You may have even overlooked an asset that you own. In any of these cases, it is important to contact the bankruptcy trustee and have the case reopened.

If the debt should have been included in your bankruptcy case, the trustee may reopen the case and allow the debt to be entered. The process will include a meeting of the creditors involved, if needed, and further judgment on what that debt is. However, the debt cannot be new debt or debt incurred after the bankruptcy paperwork was filed. In cases where you do need to reopen a case, it is important to use a bankruptcy attorney to help you through the process. It requires filing additional, amended bankruptcy petitions, and convincing the bankruptcy trustee that the debt should have been included in your bankruptcy in the first place.

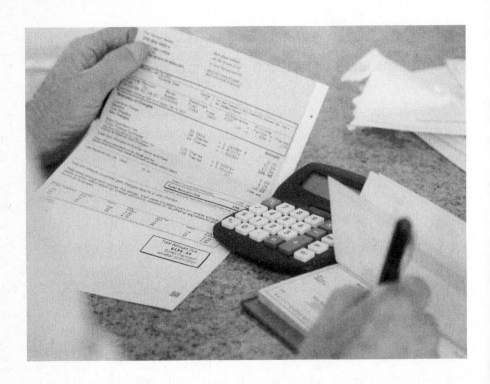

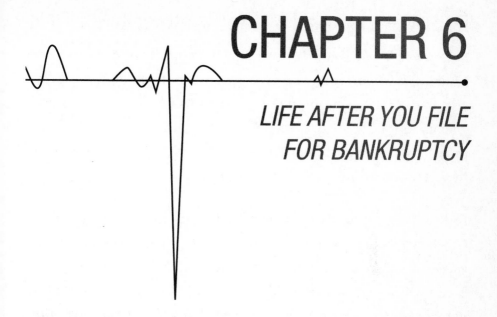

CHAPTER 6

LIFE AFTER YOU FILE FOR BANKRUPTCY

Filing for bankruptcy is a life-changing event. Not only will your credit be affected for the next decade, but you should also find yourself feeling different about spending money and your finances. You should be more conscious of monetary expenses and how you use credit. However, the first few months after bankruptcy are often filled with concern, especially when things do not go as you believe they should.

Although most of the complicated after-effects are unlikely to happen to the average bankruptcy filer, they could happen, and it is better to be prepared. This includes how to handle new or undiscovered nonexempt property and how to manage creditors after debts have been discharged. In addition, some individuals who have filed for bankruptcy might be discriminated against by employers or government agencies. It is your right to fight such occurrences.

Property Issues After Bankruptcy

After your bankruptcy discharge, your property issues should be settled. However, there are occasions when filers discover property they did not know they had, such as being listed as a beneficiary on a life insurance policy. You might also receive new property. In both situations, you need to know how to handle this property according to bankruptcy laws.

Property that is acquired soon after the discharge may cause the trustee to reopen your bankruptcy case to include such property, especially if it would be considered nonexempt property. The bankruptcy trustee is also likely to open the case if property is valuable, especially if it is likely that the property can be liquidated and the funds used to repay your creditors. However, it is best for you to disclose all property you receive or purchase within the first 180 days after your bankruptcy to your bankruptcy trustee, even if it does not have substantial value to it. The decision of whether to open the bankruptcy case again is up to the trustee, not you.

You will need to alert the trustee of any property you acquire within 180 days after you file for bankruptcy or in any situation in which you become entitled to receive property, such as being added to a life insurance policy. Be sure to include any type of property you inherit during this time. Include divorce settlements you receive. Report any disbursements from life insurance policies or any death benefit plan you may receive during that 180 days after your filing date.

To report this new property, simply file a Supplemental Schedule and the Proof of Service form, which is available in the same place you obtained the bankruptcy forms to fill out to file. Then, submit any documentation you have of the property ownership (a photocopy of it) to the court along with the form. You should keep a copy of this information for your own records.

If you fail to alert the bankruptcy trustee that you have acquired or have become entitled to receiving such property and the trustee learns of it, the trustee can ask the court to overturn your discharge, which means that your bankruptcy case will be dismissed, even if it was previously discharged. A hearing will be scheduled to make this ruling.

Debt Collectors After Bankruptcy Discharge

As mentioned, once your bankruptcy case is discharged, debt collectors no longer have the right to file any claims against you. Creditors also are forbidden from contacting you in regards to the debt. This includes any debtors that were included in the bankruptcy case specifically. If you have other creditors that were not part of the bankruptcy, or you have debts that you are still paying on because you made arrangements with the lenders to keep assets for them, those will need to be repaid. Those debt collectors can call you when necessary.

Even still, it can be hard to determine what debts you need to pay. When you get your bankruptcy discharge document, you will notice that only specific types or categories of debts (such as unsecured debts) are listed as being discharged. This document does not provide a thorough list of each creditor. This is why it can sometimes be difficult to know which lenders you need to keep paying and which lenders you no longer are responsible for.

The general rule for overcoming this dilemma is to pay any debts that were not listed in the bankruptcy as agreed. If the debt was not listed, it is unlikely the debt was discharged. Pay all new debts you incur. Your bankruptcy attorney can help you if you are still unable to make this determination. If your debt falls under any of the following types of debts, you need to repay this debt because it cannot be discharged during bankruptcy:

- Student loan debts need to be repaid, unless there is a specific court ruling that states, due to hardship, you do not have to pay the debt (you need this documentation to stop paying for student loan debts).

- Child support and alimony payments must be repaid, including any back payments you owe and all future payments.

- Taxes are not dischargeable during bankruptcy for the most part, especially those that are less than three years old or that became due in the last 240 days.

- Debts you owe as payment for personal injuries or as compensation due to an intoxication charge you were convicted of must be repaid.

- Court fees and penalties you owe to a court of law are not dischargeable.

- Most homeowner association fees need to be repaid.

- Loans from retirement accounts including pension plans, 401(k) plans, IRA's, and other forms of retirement accounts must be repaid.

Your creditors must have been given the right to file a complaint against you during the bankruptcy filings for you to legally discharge the debt. If you forgot to include a debt to a doctor, for example, in your bankruptcy petition that debt may have been discharged had you included it in your filing. However, you failed to include it, which means the doctor's collection agency did not have the ability to file a dispute in the case. Therefore, the debt is not automatically discharged. Rather than assume it is, provide documentation to the court of the debt and request the trustee reopen the bankruptcy case to include the debt.

What if the debt was discharged and the creditor is calling you? In this type of situation, you have the right to take a stand, especially if the debt collector continues to contact you. If this happens just one time, talk to the creditor and inform him or her that you have filed bankruptcy and that the debt they are trying to collect was included. Then, send a letter to the company documenting this. Here is a brief example of what you can include in your letter to a creditor that continues to contact you regarding your debt that has already been discharged by a bankruptcy court:

To Whom It May Concern,

I am writing in regard to my debt that was incurred between February 2004 and September 2008. I received a discharge for this debt through bankruptcy. My discharge occurred in December 2009. I have received numerous calls regarding this debt. Please see the bankruptcy discharge document included with this letter.

Although most debt collectors will refrain from contacting you after this point, some might continue. Sometimes minor creditors, such as a small retail store that you have a line of credit through, may not realize the extent of the law in this situation. If this continues to happen, there are several things you can do to improve the situation:

- Reopen your bankruptcy case to specifically list the creditor, if the creditor is not specifically listed on the bankruptcy documents as is. Unlisted debt is discharged in any no asset bankruptcy case. For example, if you failed to list a $400 debt from the retail store because the lender had stopped sending notices but had no assets in the bankruptcy case, that $400 was discharged even if it was not mentioned specifically on the bankruptcy documents.

- Ignore the creditor. There is no legal action that the debt collector can take at this point, when the debt is included in the bankruptcy. Therefore, if you simply ignore the debt collector, he or she may simply go away after a while. You likely have no ability to pay the debt, especially all at one time, and you legally do not have to repay any discharged debt.

In some situations, it becomes necessary to take your case, regarding continued attempts at credit collections, to court. If you feel that the creditor is simply not following the letter of the law and continues to contact you even after you have sent the creditor documentation that the debt was discharged, you can take the case to court. It is your right, and in some cases it can be important to you to defend yourself in such a way. This is especially important if the creditor is being abusive. To determine if the creditor deserves to have action taken against it, ask yourself the following questions:

- Is the creditor contacting you frequently, disrupting your day?

- Is the creditor using offensive or threatening language?

- Is the creditor legally pursuing you?

- Is the creditor contacting family members about the debt?

In any of these cases, it can be incredibly helpful to file a lawsuit against the creditor just to stop the calls. If you do proceed in this manner, use an experienced attorney to help you with the process. If you can prove the inappropriate behavior of the creditor, and that the specific debt was part of your bankruptcy, the lender may be required by the court to pay you restitution in some form, depending on the circumstances. An attorney can help you to get some type of result.

If you want to repay the debt, but you could not do so previously because of your monetary situation, you can repay it. You may want to repay the debt because it is the ethical thing to do, even though you have no obligation to do so in a court of law. However, remember that the decision is completely up to you. You can negotiate the debt with the lender, such as working out low payments. In most cases, the lender will work with you and compromise with you, especially if they have written off the debt, which means the lender no longer expects you will pay it and writes it off as a loss. However, some of the lenders are able to write off bad debts as business expenses on their taxes. If this occurs, the company might not want you to repay the debt. Contact the creditor and come up with a plan that works for you. For example, a lender's debt was discharged for $400. The lender takes a write off on his or her taxes for that amount. However, you want to repay the debt because of your religious beliefs of repaying all debt. Contact the lender first before making this payment to ensure they will accept it.

Defining the discharge

There are some situations where the discharged debt may be a bit harder to understand in terms of the creditor's current role. For example, when a creditor sues the borrower prior to the filing of bankruptcy and wins a judgment over the creditor in that case, this means a court has ruled the creditor should be paid. Although the bankruptcy may have included the debt, it will be necessary to show the creditor's judgment was discharged in the bankruptcy. If this is something that has happened to you, the best defense against such situations is to open up the bankruptcy case and ask the bankruptcy court to specifically rule that the judgment was discharged during the bankruptcy.

This is not difficult to do, as you have proven through your bankruptcy that you do not have the funds necessary to repay it. However, if you do not have this specifically listed in your bankruptcy documentation, the creditor can try to make you pay the debt years after you filed bankruptcy or years after he or she won the judgment. If a creditor wins a judgment against you, he or she can come after you once the bankruptcy is finished with documentation showing the judgment requesting you pay the money back. Therefore, if you know of any judgment against you, it is always best to ask the court to specifically state that the judgment was discharged in bankruptcy.

If the creditor has sued you and won a judgment against you either before or after the bankruptcy was settled, the creditor may have the ability to come after you for the debt. If this happens, the court is likely to rule that the creditor is able to collect funds from you through garnishment, the process of using your employer's payroll company to pull funds out of your paycheck before you even get your paycheck to repay a debt. Garnishments may only occur after a court order.

If this happens to you but you feel that the debt was in fact included in the bankruptcy, there are several things you can do. First, remember that if the creditor tries to come after your assets in this process, those assets that were exempt in your bankruptcy are still exempt right now. The creditors cannot take exempt items. A forgotten credit card, for example, might fall under this.

The creditors may be able to take up to 25 percent of your paycheck through garnishments, but not all of it. If the debt was child support or alimony, the court can rule that as much as 60 percent of your paycheck can go to repaying this debt. However, that type of debt is not dischargeable, and you will have to repay it.

To protect against garnishment in a case where you believe that the debt was covered under your bankruptcy, you must file a petition to do so with a state court (because a lower, bankruptcy court ruled in favor of the creditor). This is simply an appeals process, and this will be a challenge; therefore, you should enlist the help of a bankruptcy attorney. Nevertheless, if the debt was discharged, you can fight the case. The state court will schedule a hearing, during which you will present your evidence of the bankruptcy and your belief that the debt has been discharged. You may also have to show that repayment of the debt, especially through garnishments, is too difficult for you by explaining your income and expenses. The state court will then determine if you should have to repay the debt or not.

As mentioned earlier, some debts are unable to be discharged in bankruptcy. If you are facing garnishment because of those debts, it may be necessary to repay the debt. This includes taxes, child support, and alimony. The federal government can garnish as much as 100 percent of your wages to repay a federal tax owed, such as your federal income tax. In situations like this, there simply is not going to be a legal defense against stopping the garnishment altogether. You owe the money. You have failed to pay the money, and as a direct result, a court ruled in favor of garnishing your wages. However, this does not mean you have no options. You can try to work with the owed party to lower the amount paid per month or per pay period. Rather than defending yourself as being unable to pay at all, present to the court an option of what you can pay. The court is likely to lower the payment to a reasonable level, because you are making an effort to repay the debt. If the owed party (such as the federal government) does not work directly with you to lower the amount of a garnishment, take the case to the court it came from for some type of compromise.

Fighting clearly discharged debts

In cases where the debt was discharged and specifically mentioned in bankruptcy papers as such, you should fight the requirement to repay the debt that a creditor or a court is trying to collect. Here is what you can do to fight such discharged debts:

- If the debt was listed specifically on your bankruptcy documents, you can assume that it was discharged, unless the bankruptcy discharge document you received clearly stated it was not.

- If you had a no asset case and failed to list a creditor, you can also assume it was discharged in a bankruptcy because you had no assets for lenders to collect from.

- If you did not list a creditor in a no asset case and that creditor is filing a complaint against you, ask the judge to reopen the bankruptcy case and specifically list the debt within it. This should be no problem, but there needs to be an opportunity for the creditor to claim why it believes you should have to pay. The bankruptcy court will usually rule in your favor.

- Keep paying on non-dischargeable debts.

- If a creditor comes after you in an asset-based bankruptcy case and the debt was not listed in the bankruptcy paperwork, reopen the bankruptcy case and ask the court to rule in the discharge of the debt. Chances are good that all assets have been liquidated and paid to other creditors anyway, so the new creditor is unlikely to be able to obtain anything from your case. They cannot collect if there is nothing to collect from.

In cases where the debt is listed in the bankruptcy and it was discharged, the law states that creditors may not file a lawsuit against you, send you any type of letters about filing a lawsuit, or send collection letters demanding to be paid. The creditor cannot call you. The creditor cannot threaten you. The creditor is unable to file any type of criminal complaint against you.

In situations like this, send another letter to the creditor with more stern and specific language. Include the following:

- List your name, address, account number (if you have it), and the amount you owe.

- State that you have contacted the creditor in the past regarding the discharge of your debt (hence, this is a second letter).

- State that the debt was discharged in bankruptcy and include a copy of the discharge statement with your letter.

- Make this statement as well: "As per federal law, 11 U.S.C. § 524, your company is in violation of bankruptcy law because of your collection efforts on a discharged debt."

- State your next step should the debts collection efforts continue, which should be to pursue legal rights through the aid of an attorney who may bring harassment charges against the creditor.

- Make more than one copy of this letter for you and your attorney's records. Further, if the harassment is significant, allow your attorney to draft the letter on your behalf to ensure that it is legally binding.

The collection efforts should stop immediately. If not, contact an attorney and sue the creditor for harassment. In this type of lawsuit, the creditor may be found in contempt of court, because the bankruptcy discharge is an act of the court and the creditors are violating that order. In some cases, the court may levy a hefty fine on the creditor, which may be to due to the humiliation, inconvenience, or other turmoil the creditor caused you by trying to collect on this debt. The creditor may also be ordered to pay your attorney's fees.

This type of lawsuit can be brought to a state court or a bankruptcy court. In most situations, the bankruptcy court is the best choice, because these courts have a solid understanding and precedent for collection efforts after discharge, where the state court may draw out the process. Use your attorney's guidance in filing this type of lawsuit.

Is it worth the legal hassle to go through this process? If the creditor is harassing you and this is disrupting your quality of life in some way, then yes, it is well worth the work. However, there is no guarantee you will be awarded money for your trouble and, therefore, you should not go after the creditor in this manner if they sent you a single letter to collect the debt. If your goal is to make money off of the creditor's misbehavior, it may not be worth the effort. The costs alone may be expensive, not to mention your time investment.

Revocation of discharge

There are some circumstances when someone, such as a creditor or a bankruptcy trustee, may try to revoke the bankruptcy discharge ruling. This may occur, for example, if the trustee learns you have undisclosed assets that could have been liquidated to repay your lenders. If the discharge is "revoked," this means all of the debts included in your bankruptcy become your legal requirement to repay again. This is a rare occurrence, though it is more likely to be successful if the bankruptcy trustee files for revocation rather than a creditor doing so, for example, because the court will believe you are attempting to abuse the bankruptcy process.

If this occurs, it is strongly recommended you hire a bankruptcy attorney to fight the revocation. An attorney is necessary because there is a reason why such a claim has been brought before the bankruptcy court, and if the court has ruled that a hearing is necessary, this could signal that there is some merit to the case. A bankruptcy attorney can help protect your bankruptcy status.

In order for a creditor or the trustee to have your debt revoked, the prosecution must have some type of proof that one of the following situations occurred:

- There was some type of fraud you were guilty of that affects your bankruptcy case, such as being misleading in your documents. The discovery of fraud may occur after the bankruptcy case is discharged if a complaint is filed.

- You failed to answer an important question during the bankruptcy case or in some other way refused to obey the order of the bankruptcy court before the bankruptcy was discharged. This may be discovered after the bankruptcy was discharged if a complaint is filed.

- You intentionally failed to inform the bankruptcy trustee that you received property, which should have been included in your bankruptcy estate. This includes property you received through an inheritance, a divorce settlement, or other similar types of accusations. Any type of property like this must be added to your assets, if you acquired that property within 180 days after filing your bankruptcy papers.

There are a few other protections in place here. For the creditor or the trustee to use fraud as a reason for the revocation of your bankruptcy, the evidence and the charges must be brought before the bankruptcy court within one year of your discharge. After that point, no revocation can occur. If there is a claim that you failed to provide specific information, the charge must be brought within one year of your discharge, or it may be brought while the bankruptcy case remains open.

You will be alerted of any situation in which there is a complaint against you through a letter in the mail. It is rare that the bankruptcy trustee will call you, but this may occur as well. The mailed document will provide you with a date of the scheduled meeting to determine if the complaint is valid and whether the bankruptcy discharge should be revoked. Use an attorney to fight the specific charge. If the court does rule that there is sufficient cause and revokes the discharge, you will owe all of your debts to the lenders, even if those lenders had nothing to do with the revocation. If you have made payments through the trustee toward those creditors, such as surrendering property, your accounts with specific creditors and lenders are credited that amount, though you must pay anything more than that amount.

Discrimination After Bankruptcy

Some might think they will never own property again, but that does not need to be the case. Bankruptcy laws help to protect you even after you file for bankruptcy. This includes fighting against discrimination from the government and from non-government organizations. Specifically, all governments, including federal, state, and local governments, are unable to deny, revoke, or suspend any type of permit, charter, license, grant, or something similar on the sole fact that you filed for bankruptcy. Under bankruptcy code, specifically under 11 U.S.C. § 525(a), you are protected from many adverse conditions. However, this does not provide you with complete protection.

Bankruptcy code does not protect you from discrimination when it comes to obtaining loans. If you apply for a government loan or you request a government-provided extension of credit, there is no protection to you. The lender has the right to say "no" based on your bankruptcy filing. However, the bankruptcy code does protect you from being excluded from government guaranteed student loan programs based on your bankruptcy.

You will also be protected from the following under bankruptcy law:

- The government cannot deny you a job based on your bankruptcy or fire you from a current government job you hold based solely on your bankruptcy.

- You cannot lose your public benefits or be evicted from public housing based solely on your bankruptcy.

- You cannot be refused renewal of a liquor license based solely on your bankruptcy.

- Your college transcript cannot be withheld from you based solely on your bankruptcy.

- You cannot be denied a driver's license based solely on your bankruptcy.

- You cannot be kept from applying for, or getting, a government contract project based solely on your bankruptcy.

Additionally, your discharged debts can no longer be used to stop you from obtaining the same benefits again. If you failed to pay a debt from your driver's license suspension, for example, and the bankruptcy discharged those debts, you can now get your driver's license again. It is useful to remember: If the bankruptcy did not discharge the debt owed to the government agency, filing for bankruptcy does not give you the right to obtain those benefits again. You will have to repay the non-discharged debt before you can use the government benefit again. If you are not sure if the debt was discharged, you can have the bankruptcy court reopen your bankruptcy case to make a formal judgment on the debt, especially if you and the government agency disagree on the discharge of the debt.

In addition, these conditions only provide you with protection from bankruptcy discrimination. You may still be denied these benefits if you do not meet other qualifications, such as income requirements or even creditworthiness.

When You Need Help

This book provides you with most of the information you need to file for bankruptcy. However, it may not be enough for you. There are circumstances when you need additional help, such as complex situations involving taxes, and there are going to be times when using the aid of an attorney is simply the easiest — and most important — decision you can make.

There is a great deal of bankruptcy information out there, and not every case can be completely explained within the pages of this book. The good news is, for the self-filer, there are other resources you can use for more complicated bankruptcy situations.

If you need help filling out bankruptcy forms or typing petitions, use **bankruptcy petition preparers**, who provide services through the bankruptcy courts. They will provide you with information regarding your exemptions and will provide you with information about the tax consequences of filing for bankruptcy. They can also help with reaffirmations of debt and help you to determine what assets are part of your bankruptcy case. These facilities also provide you with bankruptcy procedure help and general information. They do not physically handle the submission of bankruptcy documents or represent you in a court of law, however. Fees charged by bankruptcy petition preparers are capped. The maximum charge for these services is $150. You can also use law libraries and the Internet to help with complex situations. Choose bankruptcy court Web sites or attorney Web sites for researching such services.

In many cases, hiring an attorney is the best option. You will find numerous lawyers in each of the bankruptcy districts who can help you to prepare your case. Further, you will find a wide range of them offering very affordable services. Attorneys know you do not have much money to spend on attorney fees when you are filing for bankruptcy. If you do hire an attorney, look for one who is willing to allow you to prepare your own case, if you want to. There is not a rule stating that you have to file for bankruptcy with an attorney, and even if you hire one, you may only need advice. Some people simply want to remain in legal control of their case. Seek out an attorney willing of offer guidance and information without actually handling the filing of the case, if this is what you want. *More information on bankruptcy attorneys can be found in Chapter 2.*

Any company or organization you pay to help you in any way with your bankruptcy is called a "debt relief agency" under bankruptcy laws. These companies or organizations must identify themselves as debt relief agencies under law. This does not include credit counseling agencies or budget counselors. Bankruptcy law places strict requirements on these agencies.

Debt relief agencies

Any debt relief agency must provide you with a contract within five days of working with you that states specifically what services the agency will provide and what those services will cost. These contracts must fully provide the terms of payment as well. If you agree to work with the agency, you need to sign the contract, and the agency must then provide you with a copy.

In addition, there are disclosures and notices the debt relief agencies must provide to you. The agency must tell you that all information you provide in your bankruptcy paperwork must be complete, truthful, and accurate to the best of your knowledge. The agency must also provide you with notice that you have to fully discuss all of your assets and liabilities and document this in your bankruptcy paperwork as defined by law.

Before you write down the value of any asset, you must learn what the replacement cost of that asset is. The agency provides a disclosure stating that all information regarding your income, including all information you provide to determine a means test, must be accurate and placed in your bankruptcy papers only after the agency has made reasonable inquiry into the accuracy of this information.

In addition, a disclosure is provided to you stating that your bankruptcy case may be audited, and if you fail to cooperate with such an audit, your bankruptcy case may be dismissed at any time. You can also be held criminally responsible for any false claims you make. These disclosures are meant to provide you with the most important requirements placed on you. Further, the agency also must provide you with options regarding your bankruptcy and must also provide you with a list of requirements you must meet in order to file for bankruptcy.

Even more importantly, the information a debt relief agency supplies must be easy to understand and accurate. However, there are some restrictions placed on debt relief agencies that you need to know about before you begin working with them. For example, you should know that once the agency provides you with information on what it will do for you, it has to do so. The agency may not tell you to make a statement on your bankruptcy petition that is inaccurate, misleading, or fraudulent in another manner. It must not encourage you to be anything but truthful on these documents.

In addition, the debt relief agency cannot encourage you to incur more debt before you file for bankruptcy. Before the new bankruptcy laws went into effect in 2005, it was somewhat common for a bankruptcy attorney or other agency to simply tell the individual that he or she could use his or her credit cards up to the credit limit before they filed. Some would encourage people to max out their credit cards. This is no longer allowable. The agency is unable to tell you that you can obtain more credit or recommend you do so.

The cost of working with a debt relief agency is left up to the agency to determine. However, there are restrictions. The U.S. trustee will review all fees charged by these agencies to ensure the fee is reasonable.

Who needs a lawyer

Do you need a bankruptcy petition preparer or do you need a lawyer? It is always an option to hire an attorney to help you with your bankruptcy petition. If you answer any of the following questions with "yes," you should consider hiring an attorney before you file a bankruptcy petition.

- Do you have a home or other assets that could be at risk of being liquidated to repay creditors, but you want to keep that property?

- Is your income too high over the last six months to qualify you for Chapter 7 bankruptcy, but you believe circumstances still help you to qualify for it?

- Have you recently given property or other assets away and are concerned that this may disqualify you from filing Chapter 7 bankruptcy?

- Have you sold property for less than what it was worth in the last year?

- Do you want to get your bankruptcy discharge to include questionable debt, such as old tax debt, student loans, or other judgments filed against you in the past?

- Are you facing a lawsuit that a creditor has filed against one or more of your assets?

- Is the bankruptcy trustee or a creditor trying to have your bankruptcy case dismissed for some reason?

- Is the bankruptcy trustee or a creditor trying to have your case revoked after a discharge has been given to you?

- Do you think that a Chapter 13 bankruptcy repayment plan will be too difficult for you to manage financially?

- Are you trying to stop foreclosure?

- Is a creditor asking the court to allow the creditor to continue to collect on a debt that you think should have been included in the bankruptcy discharge?

- Are you facing harassments from creditors after you have filed for bankruptcy or after your bankruptcy discharge has occurred?

- Do you find yourself in legal trouble because you have spent too much money in recent months either to qualify to file for bankruptcy or during the bankruptcy? Have you spent a great deal of money within 180 days of your bankruptcy filing date?

- Are you trying to negotiate your debt with your creditor and need help?

If there are any other complications in your bankruptcy case, consider hiring an attorney to help you with the process. This can alleviate a great deal of difficulty for you, and it may even help you to get through the bankruptcy quickly and without any risk of dismissal of your case. Any time you have questions regarding a bankruptcy case, an attorney is the best source of information and guidance.

CASE STUDY: EVERY CASE IS DIFFERENT

David Leibowitz
Practicing Attorney
www.lakelaw.com

Practicing attorney David Leibowitz offers insight and explanation into the bankruptcy process from years of experience. For ten years, he has provided bankruptcy aid for consumers and businesses alike. He offers a variety of advice for anyone considering bankruptcy:

If you are thinking of filing a bankruptcy case, you probably need to do so. You are probably being hounded by your creditors in collection or getting your wages garnished. In general, do not try to do it yourself. Get competent counsel. Look for an attorney certified by the American Board of Certification (**www.abcworld.org**) or an attorney who is a member of National Association of Consumer Bankruptcy Attorneys. There are other fine attorneys in the consumer field too, but these are two good indicators. Very good information for consumers is available at the Web site of the American Bankruptcy Institute (**www.abi.org**).

Every case is unique. Difficult cases require more preparation, but the basic analysis is similar in all cases. What are the assets? What are the liabilities? What is exempt? What has the debtor done in the past? Disclosure is vital, and not all debtors either want to disclose or know what must be disclosed. Getting to the truth is vital, even if the client does not want to disclose everything. Sometimes, we have to turn a client away if the client wants not to disclose.

There are sometimes questions of whether a particular debt may be discharged in bankruptcy. This can lead to litigation. There are sometimes questions of whether pre-petition transfers can be avoided. This can also lead to litigation. Basically, I try to get the facts, disclose them as well as possible, anticipate problems, and try to avoid them.

If the unexpected happens, we respond to it. We go to court if necessary. We contest creditors' and others' motions. This is more of an exception than a rule. Bankruptcy is full of traps for the unwary. A case can be dismissed for failure to get proper credit counseling, for failure to file tax returns or pay advices (pay stubs or proof of income), if filed within eight years of a prior bankruptcy, or if schedules are not filed properly or timely. Discharge can be denied if the debtor fails to take financial management. A debtor can file for bankruptcy himself or herself. But then again, I suppose one can fix one's own brakes on a car. The problem is that if you mess up, the consequences can be severe.

PART 2

Small Business Bankruptcy

Just as consumers can file for bankruptcy, so can businesses. As a business owner, deciding if you need to file for bankruptcy is a complex process best done with the help of an attorney. However, bankruptcy can help you to realign your business debts or help you successfully close the doors on a failing business.

According to the Automated Access to Court Electronic Records (ACER), there were 36,103 small business bankruptcy filings filed in the first five months of 2009. That is a 52 percent increase from 2008, when 23,829 small businesses filed. Estimates state that there are 350 small businesses that fail each day in the United States, with most of these using Chapter 11 as a way of restructuring their debts.

According to the U.S. Small Business Administration, about 50 percent of all small businesses fail within the first five years of being in operation. There are many reasons that these businesses fail, such as poor financial management or bad business decisions, but many of them will need to turn to bankruptcy as a way of either getting some of their debt discharged or to reorganize the debt to make it easier to repay. For many, bankruptcy is the best route to take.

CHAPTER 7

SMALL BUSINESS BANKRUPTCY EXPLAINED

Small business bankruptcy is similar to consumer bankruptcy in that many of the procedures are the same. However, you are dealing with a business rather than a single person (or married couple), and therefore, there are likely more people involved and more concerns for filing this type of bankruptcy. Small business bankruptcy is available to those who are hoping to liquidate the debt they have within their business. By liquidating the debt, the business owner is no longer responsible for it.

One of the first things you need to take into consideration is whether you need to use an attorney to file for bankruptcy as a small business. Although the law does not require having an attorney, it is important to know that doing so can be incredibly helpful in ensuring the process is fast and efficient. Some bankruptcy courts simply do not have the means, time, or patience to work with businesses that want to represent themselves.

As with consumer bankruptcy, there are federal laws and state laws you must follow when filing for bankruptcy on behalf of your business. There are often local laws as well. Hiring an attorney helps ensure you meet all requirements in your area. Whether or not you decide to use an attorney, this section of the book will guide you through the process of filing for bankruptcy as a small business owner. *Chapter 1 outlined what bankruptcy is and which laws govern it.* This section defines the specific differences between small business bankruptcy and consumer bankruptcy.

Types of Businesses

Do you know what type of business you have? Many small business owners are not sure of the legal steps involved in defining the type of business he or she has, but this does play a role in how your business can file for bankruptcy. For example, just because you place the word "company" in your business name, does not mean that you have a corporation. If you are unsure of your legal status as a business, contact your accountant or tax professional. The type of business you have directly affects the type of bankruptcy your company can file; therefore, it is critical to know this information.

Sole proprietorships

By far, the most common type of small business is the sole proprietorship. Any sized business can be a sole proprietorship. In fact, your business is likely a sole proprietorship even if you have never defined it as such or anything else. Other types of businesses, such as limited liability companies and corporations, must be legally defined as such through application to the government.

From the time you start operating your business, it is called a sole proprietorship.

Sole proprietorship is a legal term used to describe an individual operating a business without any special status. You did not have to file legal documentation for this classification. Under this type of law, the business's debts are the personal debts of the business owner. The business's assets can be used to satisfy the individual's personal debts, too. Legally, there is no distinction between a person and the business itself, which means the bankruptcy process is very similar. One of the mistakes individuals make with this type of business is to sell off his or her assets and have a false belief that creditors cannot come after personal property (property not associated with the business) to settle those debts. Because there is no legal distinction here, business assets can be used to repay personal creditors and personal assets can be used to pay business creditors. This is simply how property ownership is defined in this type of business. Your home's equity could be used to repay business debt; your business's equipment may be sold to repay your personal debt.

Partnerships

A partnership occurs when two or more people agree to operate a business together. The two or more people do not have to file for any type of special status with the government. A partnership is formed at the moment two people agree on how to split profits from the business. This may be done through an oral agreement or through a written agreement. Both are legally binding. Oral agreements are often legally binding when you can show they occurred, such as showing that a business partner provided money to start the business.

All partners are responsible for all of the business's debts, even with their personal assets. A creditor can go after one or more of the partners and his or her assets to repay a debt. The partnership does not allow for the formation of any type of protection for the personal property of each of the partners. It is not a legal separation from personal property and property rights. As you may be able to tell, this leaves every partner in the business vulnerable to the actions and debts of other partners. Even if one partner does not know about the debt incurred by another partner, he or she can be held responsible for that debt within the business. Partnerships can place your business at stake in conjunction with your partner's financial debts, but your personal debts are not affected unless they tie into your business in some way.

Corporations

Although sole proprietorships are the most common form of small business, when considering legal business status (which requires documents to be legally filed to form the business), the corporation is the most common form of business. This type of business structure protects shareholders within the business from liability of corporate debt. The corporation is a separate entity, prohibiting creditors from collecting outside of the business. In order to be a corporation, the business needs to meet the requirements of the state where it operates most of its business. Each state has minimal operational guidelines for the business to meet, such as electing a board of directors.

Although becoming a corporation is not difficult, the creditors of a small business will want to have some type of personal guarantee of the debt from the small business owner to ensure that if the business fails, the owner will still repay the debt owed. The creditors may go to the business owner to require this type of guarantee. The business owner needs to be very careful about signing such contracts from creditors. Signing the debt with your name could mean that you will be held responsible for the debt. To avoid this type of personal liability, ensure that these contracts specifically state that the business solely is responsible for the debt. This should always be the case within your business.

Limited liability companies

Limited liability companies, or LLCs, are the newest form of business legal organization. This type of organization gives the business owner the limited liability he or she is seeking and helps the business to avoid double taxation. Limited liability simply means that your personal assets are not at risk if your business files bankruptcy or fails. For tax purposes, the LLC is treated the same as a sole proprietorship or a partnership, but it still provides the owner with a corporate shield of protection from the business's debt. As with corporations, the small-business owner must ensure that any contract he or she signs does not create personal liability or the owner will be held legally responsible for that debt. Reading contracts and signing them on behalf of the business is critical to limiting this type of debt responsibility.

Types of Bankruptcy

There are several types of bankruptcy available to small businesses. Chapter 13 bankruptcy is not available to the small business owner because this form is for consumers only.

Chapter 7 bankruptcy

Chapter 7 bankruptcy is an option for businesses as well as individuals. When this form of bankruptcy is filed, the debts owed and listed in the bankruptcy are wiped out. A business that uses Chapter 7 bankruptcy may lose some of its assets. For example, if a business owns substantial real estate, the bankruptcy court may require that some of the real estate be sold to repay a portion of the debt. Unlike consumers filing for Chapter 7 bankruptcy, small business assets are not protected by exemptions, and the business is likely to lose equipment and other assets if not paid for. Many of these assets are secured debts and can be continued to be paid, which would allow the business to maintain those assets throughout the bankruptcy filing.

Chapter 11 bankruptcy

Although Chapter 11 bankruptcy is the option that many large businesses use, it is not always a good option for the small-business owner. One of the biggest disadvantages to filing Chapter 11 bankruptcy for the small business is the cost. The costs range greatly but can be in the thousands of dollars, depending on the size of the organization and the amount of work the attorney needs to do. This particular type of bankruptcy allows for the owner to stop collections from creditors. It allows for the business to renegotiate fixed contracts and to get rid of unprofitable assets in an orderly manner. However, this is not usually a benefit to the small business-owner with a single-store operation, because you likely do not have fixed contractors nor multiple properties and assets to dispose of.

Chapter 11 bankruptcy is best suited for large businesses such as manufacturers or large, multi-store retailers. In this type of bankruptcy, the creditors' lawyers will come into court in an effort to protect the creditors. They will try to defend the contracts the business took on. They will state the creditors' needs and try to convince the courts to require the debt be repaid. The business continues to operate but does so under the direction of the court, though the management of the business usually stays in place. You will need to file periodic reports to the courts and creditors to show the current state of the business's financial health. Third-party accountants specializing in bankruptcy cases are required too and must be approved by the courts.

In Chapter 11 bankruptcy, a reorganization plan is established. This plan outlines who the creditors are and places them in classes based on the types of loan they provided, with secured loans taking precedence over unsecured debts. The plan establishes which creditors will be paid first and how much. The plan is then presented to the creditors for a vote. This is very different from Chapter 7 bankruptcy, where the creditors have no say in the bankruptcy proceedings. If most of the creditors agree, then the plan is approved. Because of this complex process, Chapter 11 bankruptcy is best suited for large businesses.

Chapter 12 bankruptcy

The next type of bankruptcy chapter your business could file is Chapter 12 bankruptcy. However, this is a very specific type of bankruptcy that is linked only to those who operate a farm. The farm has a unique business model as the sale of crops or animals usually occurs only once a year, but farmers still have monthly bills to pay. If you own a farm, this specialized type of bankruptcy could fit your particular needs.

Chapter 13 bankruptcy

Chapter 13 is an option for small businesses that have a steady income and can repay their debts but need more time to do so. It is different from Chapter 11 bankruptcy as it does not have as much oversight by the courts, nor as much involvement from creditors. In this type of plan, the profits left over after all the business's expenses are paid are then applied to pay back the debt owed. The funds are paid to the trustee in the case, who will then pay the creditors according to the plan put in place.

In choosing the right type of bankruptcy for your business, it becomes important to consider numerous factors, starting with your goals for your business. A business owner who is willing to give up some personal assets and business assets should consider Chapter 7 bankruptcy. If the business owner wants to continue running the business, the only options available are Chapter 11 and Chapter 13 bankruptcy, of which Chapter 11 bankruptcy is simply unrealistic. In most situations, small-business owners have to turn to Chapter 13 bankruptcy if they hope to keep their businesses operational beyond bankruptcy.

Mingling of business and personal debt

In most small businesses, there is interplay between personal debt and business debt. For example, to start your business, you often need to turn to a lender to request a personal loan; you need to order supplies, and you need to establish your business — all of which you need funds to do. With such a new business, creditors generally do not loan unless they get a personal guarantee from you that you will pay for the loan even if your business fails. A creditor may require some type of security, for example, such as a loan against your home. This causes the personal and business debt to be intermingled. Some people will have the ability to obtain unsecured loans from lenders because they have sufficient credit to do so. However, most people will need to use some type of asset, such as their home or business equipment, as a way of guaranteeing the borrowed funds will be repaid. In the case of a lease on a building, most landlords require that the individual sign the lease rather than putting it in a company's name.

There are other situations in which personal and business debt become entwined. If a business hits a rough spot, the business owner may use his or her collateral to help reestablish the business. In some cases, the business owner might begin using business vehicles for personal use, which is discouraged in most situations. In these situations, it becomes difficult for the business's assets and debts to be differentiated from the individual's debts.

Often, this mix of personal and business debt leads to the individual needing to file for bankruptcy for both his or her personal debt and his or her business debt. Many business owners are faced with complex financial problems like this as a direct result of mixing these debts. Whenever possible, they should be kept separated to ensure that your business does not affect your personal finances.

Can Your Business Avoid Bankruptcy?

If you are at the point of considering bankruptcy for your business, you might think there is no other option. But, there may be alternatives.

The first step in the process is to create a budget for your business and to stick to it. Bringing down expenses is an excellent way to keep your business running without having to file for bankruptcy. Cutting spending is something that business owners need to do on a regular basis, even if they are not facing bankruptcy. If a budget is in place and you are still struggling with financial problems, the next step is to consider borrowing or debt consolidation.

One thing that makes business creditors different from personal creditors is that with most business creditors, you need to keep a good, working relationship with them so that they continue to provide you with the supplies you need to operate your business. If you stop paying the company that supplies your restaurant with bread products, you no longer have bread to serve to your customers. You need to keep a good relationship with these organizations to ensure they keep supplying to you.

Because of this, many business owners turn to other sources of money to borrow and to consolidate the debt they owe to avoid letting business debts go unpaid. Many business owners turn to their homes as a source of borrowing potential. If you have equity in your home, you may be able to borrow against that equity to pay down other debts. Before you do this, remember three things:

1. Never borrow against your home to pay unsecured debts, such as credit card payments. You are securing these loans by doing so, which means that the home must be sold for you to clear the debt or the loan needs to be repaid.

2. Never wait too long for a creditor to confirm a home equity loan. It should not take more than one or two weeks. If it takes longer than this, the lender is not being honest with you.

3. Realize that many loan brokers (those who match up borrowers with lenders) are only concerned with their profit, not your best interest. If you are going to borrow against your home, get quotes from several places and compare them carefully.

Another option to consider is borrowing against a retirement fund, though this is rarely a good thing for your business. If you do borrow against your retirement fund, you might need to pay a hefty fine for pulling money out of the fund early. This could amount to your current income tax rate plus a penalty fee of 10 percent. In addition to this, you may find that borrowing against your retirement is costing you even more: the compounding interest that occurs year after year. These funds are meant for your retirement and if you borrow against them, you can starve your retirement plan of that interest.

Working out a plan with your creditors may be an option for you. However, you will need to work with them on a one-on-one basis to find a solution that works. It is often the case that small-business creditors are less likely to close off your credit if you work to find a solution, because they want to keep loaning to turn a profit. If you are dealing with creditors keep these tips in mind:

- Ensure that you are providing creditors with the truth. Explain your circumstances so they realize you are doing your best to pay down the debt.

- Take note of any information they provide you. If a creditor agrees to specific terms, ensure you get this information in writing before making payments. Creditors are in the business of getting you to pay; they are not working for you.

- Creditors cannot threaten you in any way. They cannot make false promises, either. Instruct creditors to provide you with an official letter in the mail regarding their offer if you are skeptical about what they are offering.

Working with creditors is difficult, and many people simply cannot meet the demands that several creditors make. This is why many people will end up filing for bankruptcy rather than struggling to try repaying creditors over several years.

Trade creditors

If you own the type of business that has credit accounts with businesses who provide you with regular service or supplies, you can often work out a deal with these organizations in a more effective manner than with other creditors because they see the benefit in doing so. These types of creditors are called trade creditors. Most often, they are more willing to work with you, because these organizations realize the true benefit in doing so. For example, if you owe them $5,000 for the perishable goods for your store, and your lender stops supplying you with those goods to resell, there is little chance you will be able to turn a profit to pay them any of the $5,000 back. Instead, these organizations often will agree to a cash-on-delivery style of business arrangement. They would rather do this than lose business.

Most trade creditors also realize that if they are too harsh with you about repaying your past due debt, you could just turn to another creditor to get these resources anyway. The original creditor then becomes less of your priority because you are more likely to stay current with a new creditor. It is unlikely the new creditor would have knowledge of your relationship with the old creditor. If the new creditor did, he or she might offer a cash-on-delivery system from the start of the relationship with the business.

Working out debt repayment

A third-party debt negotiator or resource is the next option for you. If you find that working one-on-one with your creditors is simply too hard to do, you can call in a third party to provide you with assistance in this process. Doing so can be an excellent result if you have the means to repay some of the debt but need a plan to help you get there.

A workout program, as it is often called, is a deal that is brokered by a third party between the creditor and the business owner. In some cases, these organizations can be helpful, though you may want to try to work through trade creditors. A workout program may be necessary for your business; it may also be necessary for your personal debt. If that is the case, you may need to use these services to help you separate the two and help you to repay all of your debts, both personal and business related, at the same time.

One of the most common types of third-party organizations for this is a consumer credit-counseling agency. Some of these agencies work strictly with businesses to help the business owner restructure debt to make it easier to repay. Other companies, called debt-consolidation companies or debt-settlement companies, are other solutions. Credit counseling agencies can set up monthly payments from you to lenders that are more affordable for you. These organizations collect your money until you have enough to offer a settlement to the creditor as payment in full. This money is placed in an account until it accumulates enough.

If these organizations claim to be nonprofit, verify this information is accurate before you use the service. Nonprofit organizations often charge less for their services. Find out what fees are charged, as well as how the debts are repaid. If the organization collects payments from you and places them in an account to pay creditors at a later time, keep in mind that the creditors will continue to collect against you until the debt is repaid. Plus, there is no guarantee that a creditor will agree to work with these third-party organizations. They may in fact pull out of any plan these third parties put in place at any time, leaving you without a way to repay the debt. They may do this, for example, because they want to pursue other collection methods or even sell the debt to another organization.

Making the Decision to File for Bankruptcy

Although there are methods to use to help you to avoid bankruptcy, it is quite important for you to consider bankruptcy and its benefits. *Review the options to avoid bankruptcy listed in Chapter 1 of this book.* However, if you have worked through these and are still struggling to find a solution that works for your unique situation, bankruptcy will be your next option.

If you file Chapter 13 bankruptcy for your small business, you will have several key benefits:

1. You will be able to keep your business operational. Any small business that has the potential to be profitable can be kept open. However, you should take the time to find out if your business can turn a profit. If the business does not have a profit left over after all expenses are paid on a month-to-month basis, the business may not be viable. Your accountant can help you to examine these factors.

2. The Chapter 13 bankruptcy plan will force all collection activity, garnishments, and foreclosures to stop. This automatic stay will last through the Chapter 13 bankruptcy process. This can help keep your business's assets intact.

3. The Chapter 13 bankruptcy plan will also help force your creditors to work with you. For example, if your business cannot handle the $1,000 payment toward an unsecured lender, a bankruptcy plan can help you get that payment lowered to $500.

4. A Chapter 13 bankruptcy may help you to reduce your debts. The bankruptcy trustee may reduce unsecured debts, such as credit card loans, if it is deemed necessary to keep your business operational.

5. Secured debts, such as your home, real estate, and business equipment, continue to be paid off fully through a Chapter 13 plan, unless you decide to give these properties back to the lender.

There are some key benefits to filing for Chapter 13 bankruptcy, but for some businesses it becomes necessary to fold. As mentioned, if your business does not have a positive number after all expenses are paid off monthly, it may not be possible for the business to remain in operation. Here is how to determine this:

- Determine what your monthly income is, including any receipts for sales and accounts receivable.

- Add up all expenses for your business. This includes inventory costs and expenses for running the business, such as rental payments, utilities, and payroll.

- Subtract all expenses from your accounts receivable.

- If this number is negative, your business does not have the sales to turn a profit.

- If this number is positive, your business has a profit that can be used to pay down debt.

If your business is operating at a loss, you may be able to look for ways to trim your budget, such as reducing your labor or discontinuing expensive services that are costing you too much. A cost analysis of your business will help you see areas of opportunity here.

It can be a hard decision to make to close your business, but in some situations, it becomes necessary to do so. The market might not be right or the competition might be too steep. You may find that larger competitors are too hard to compete with or that payroll costs and taxes are too high in your area. In cases where you cannot turn a profit, shuttering the doors to your business may be the best route for you to take personally, rather than funneling more money into your budget.

Unless you can sell your business's assets to repay any debts you owe, filing for Chapter 7 becomes very important. Otherwise, these creditors can come after your personal assets to repay your business debts unless your business is protected through its legal status. Further, if your personal debt and business debts are intermixed with each other, consider the value of filing for Chapter 7 bankruptcy for all debt. This will help free you from these burdens, and it will provide you with a fresh start.

Filing for Chapter 7 bankruptcy does not mean that you are unable to start a business again. You are free to do so, though you should make better financial decisions in accomplishing this. Focus on building up your credit for some time before you begin investing in a new business venture. Learn from past mistakes, too, such as expanding too fast or mixing your personal debt with your business debt.

One thing is for certain: With 50 percent of businesses failing within five years and most of those business owners needing to turn to bankruptcy as a way out of these debts, it is clear that bankruptcy is a solution to a problem. Consider it an opportunity to improve the financial stability of your business (if filing for Chapter 13 bankruptcy) and your personal finances. It could be just what you need to get your business back on track, too.

CHAPTER 8

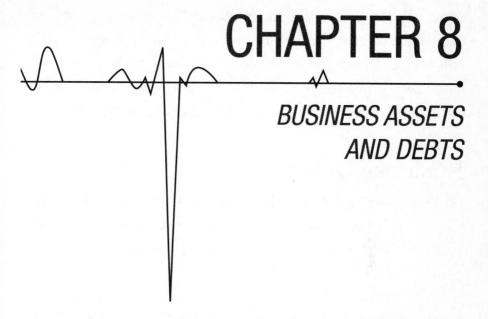

BUSINESS ASSETS AND DEBTS

As with all forms of bankruptcy, your debt — more specifically, the types of debts you have and the assets you have — are scrutinized to determine your business's qualifications for bankruptcy. One of the first steps you need to take before filing for bankruptcy is to learn what types and amounts of debt your business has and what assets the business may have that could be used to repay some or all of that debt.

It is very common for small business owners to have business debts and personal debts that are in some way tied to their business. This will affect the business bankruptcy in that case. If you borrowed money against your home to start your business or you secured personal loans in your name for your business, the bankruptcy terms may require that you liquidate those personal assets to repay business debts.

Gather your documents and work through this chapter looking for the types of debts that you have. You should note what you owe, whom you owe, and the type of debt it is (secured or unsecured). Remember that secured debt is backed by some type of valuable, such as your home, car, or business equipment. Unsecured debt is not; this type of debt is often a credit card or a personal loan where no collateral was used to obtain the loan.

Business Debts

Business debts are those debts classified as such because they have no tie to your personal finances. These are funds you borrowed using your business's name rather than against your own name.

Keep in mind that you cannot have business debts if you own a sole proprietorship or a partnership, legally. That is because these are not legal business classifications and consumer bankruptcy rules apply. In other words, there is no separation of business and personal debt in these situations. In those legal organizations of a business, all business debt is also all personal debt. There is no protection or shield from liability for you from the debts your business incurs. For the purpose of this discussion, then, business debts refer to any debts your business incurs if you have a corporation or an LLC. If you own a sole proprietorship, your liability remains intact regardless of the type of debt it is.

Real estate leases: Most small businesses do not own the property outright but rather operate in a lease agreement. Keep in mind that shutting the doors to your business does not get you off the hook for your lease contract. You may still be liable for repaying the lease even if your business is not open. It is also common for leases to be personally guaranteed, meaning you are responsible for them even if your business folds. To learn your liability here, read your lease contract.

Leases for vehicles and equipment: These leases operate the same as a real estate lease. You are likely to have to repay the debt even if the business is not operational. You may be personally responsible for repaying the lease here, unless this debt is discharged through consumer bankruptcy. Read through the lease documentation to learn if you have personal liability.

Purchase agreements: Vendor agreements or purchase agreements are those credit extensions a business secures for the purchase of supplies to operate the business. If your small business has contracts with vendors like this, you will need to learn the exact details of the contract you signed. Some organizations set up the purchase agreement in the business's name only, which may restrict liability personally to you. However, this is not always the case.

Business credit cards: Business credit cards, even if they are specifically called that, may or may not be in the business's name. It is necessary to look to the business credit card's contract to learn how much personal liability you have in these credit cards. If you signed the credit card contract with your name, you could be responsible for the debt if the business cannot cover it. If you signed the credit card as an officer of the business (for example, John James on behalf of James and Company), then you may not have personal liability.

Determine if you have any other types of debts not listed here. For each one, determine the extent of liability by examining the actual contract and the way you signed the agreement to initiate the line of credit. These factors determine if your corporation or LLC is solely responsible for the debts or if you have given a personal guarantee on the debts to the credit lenders.

Business Assets

Just as with your business debts, you also need to carefully consider your business assets, which might include everything from the money in your business bank account to the business equipment owned. Nearly all businesses have assets, and that means your business might need to repay some of your debts through liquefying its assets.

The first step in the process is to determine who owns the assets. As the small-business owner, do you own them or does the business own them solely? As with debts, this discussion applies only to those owners of corporations and LLCs, as other classifications of businesses lump assets of all types without distinction of liability.

Any asset with a title lists the owner of that asset. If the business is the titleholder, the business owns it. This is usually fairly clear on mortgages and vehicles. Other times, assets do not have an actual title to them, so it becomes more difficult to figure out who owns them. Your electronic equipment, inventory, and even your store shelves may not have a title that clearly shows ownership. They could belong to the individual or to the business, so the only way to distinguish this is to look at your documentation:

- Past receipts can be helpful in showing what type of purchase was made and by whom.

- Check your purchase agreements to determine ownership by who is listed as the responsible payer.

- Tax records may establish ownership in some items, especially if those items were depreciated for your business.

- Past checks can also provide you with more information. Was a business check or credit line used to pay for the item? Look at the actual details of ownership of those accounts to determine ownership.

It is important to establish who purchased each item and who owns it so that you can determine if it should be part of your bankruptcy filing. In corporations and LLCs, any assets you have within the business are subject to liquidation to pay off creditors under Chapter 7 bankruptcy. However, avoid trying to pass off true business assets for personal property; it is hard to say that a computer is personal property if you purchased it using a business loan.

Once you have a list of which assets you own, the next step is to determine the value of each of those items. If you have a sole proprietorship or a partnership, the value of each of these assets is critical, because you may be filing for personal bankruptcy as well as business bankruptcy. In these situations, you are able to keep a certain amount of property. However, you are only allowed a certain amount of exemptions, which is determined by the state or federal exemption rules you take. *Turn to Chapter 4 for more information on the personal exemptions that may apply here.*

If you do need to calculate the value of your assets, keep in mind that the value of your business assets is not the amount you paid for them. Depreciation is one factor that needs to be taken into consideration. When determining the value of your business assets, determine what you would likely get if you tried to sell the item today; that is the true value of the item as it stands. The only exception to this is the value of a vehicle. Rather than what you would get for selling the vehicle, the value of a vehicle is defined as the retail value of it, or what a car salesman would get if he or she were to sell the car on his or her lot. This is often significantly higher than what you may sell it for.

Determining the assets associated with your business and the assets that are strictly personal is critical before heading into bankruptcy. Once you do this, you have begun to organize your finances. Use a spreadsheet to help you with this. After you have done so, there is more to do before you can file for bankruptcy when it comes to understanding your business's financial state.

Profit and Loss Within Your Business

Many small businesses have no idea what their profits and losses are for each month or for the year. Some small businesses operate by what is called the **cigar box method** of investing, which is not necessarily a good way to operate. This term is ideal for describing how some small businesses handle their finances. When a customer makes a purchase, the money goes into the box. When there is a bill that needs to be paid, the business owner takes money out of the box to pay the bill. If the business owner needs to purchase groceries for home, he or she takes money out of the box. As you can see, this method of accounting leaves quite a bit to be desired. There is little to no actual bookkeeping being done, which could signal financial strain for any business or personal financial situation.

Why does this happen? It is not because the small business owner simply does not want to be honest about what money is coming into and out of the business. Rather, the underlying problem is often that the business owner does not have business account- ing skills or the time to invest in this process. After all, when the small-business owner is not working hands on within the busi- ness, he or she is not making money and such tasks often take away from the time the business owner is working.

Nevertheless, it is critical for all small businesses to have a grasp on what is actually happening within the finances for the busi- ness. When you are heading into bankruptcy, you need to know what the business is earning as well as what the business's ex- penses are. You also need to include the taxes that the business pays each year. A profit and loss statement is helpful. This docu- ment lists all of your assets and expenses in detail.

By determining what the business's expenses are as well as the business income, you can determine what the business has left over for your personal expenses, as well as for paying back credi- tors. Some small business owners are shocked by how little they are actually earning from the business for the amount of work they are putting into it. When you see the numbers on paper, you can clearly see if your business is able to succeed or if it simply is not possible to do this any longer.

Perform a Financial Inventory

At this point, you have taken somewhat of an inventory of what you owe to creditors. You also have taken the time to work through the assets you have. Now, it is time to consider your options.

You will need to start paying yourself if you are not already doing so to show exactly what you are taking home as payment. Rather than simply taking money from company funds, you need to give yourself a paycheck like you do any other employee. This means you should be deducting all necessary employee- and employer-related taxes, and you should be paying into a retirement fund for yourself as you would like. Even if you have not done so in the past, but rather simply took money out of the box, do this now to have proper documentation. However, if you have never used money from the business for personal needs, do not start paying yourself now.

When you perform this type of financial inventory, you establish a line between your business debt and your personal debt. Further, you ensure that there is a clear line between what is being spent on your personal expenses and your business expenses. Pay personal debts that are not related to your business through your personal accounts that are separate from your business accounts. Use these accounts strictly as they should be used, personal or business, without making purchases outside of this limitation.

Once you have done this, you can create that separation you need to start seeing what money your business is actually making and how much of your personal income and assets are involved within your business' success or failure. Some businesses pull far too much from personal assets, but in other cases, business owners use too much of a business's income for personal use. Avoid using personal assets as much as possible and ensure that any money you take as income is a justifiable amount.

The best way to find the right balance is to learn how functional the business is on the income it produces. Ask the following to determine just how functional your business is:

• Is your personal spending of business funds the problem behind your business's financial strain?

• Are you turning a profit (income minus expenses) within the business?

If you find that your business is suffering on its own because you do not have the income coming in from the business to meet the expense demands, bankruptcy is the route to go. It is only easy to see this after you have separated your finances.

Next, consider your options. If you are facing a business that is not profitable, filing Chapter 7 bankruptcy will help to reduce the debts you owe and will close the business. You may wish to file Chapter 7 to include your personal debts, too, especially if they are overly entwined with that of the business. It may be necessary to do this if you own a sole proprietorship or a partnership because there is no real separation between your business assets and debts and your personal assets and debts. *For those who have decided to go with Chapter 7 and to file personal as well as business debts, you can use the first section of this book to learn how to file for bankruptcy in detail.*

If you do have a profitable business but need help getting your debts caught up, then filing Chapter 13 bankruptcy is your best option. If you have an LLC or a corporation (by legal definition), you do not have to file personal bankruptcy to eliminate your debts. Rather, you can file for business bankruptcy under Chapter 13 instead of personal bankruptcy.

What Will You Lose?

If you file Chapter 7 bankruptcy for your business, you will lose a great deal of your business's assets, if not all of them. All the assets of the business are collected by the trustee of the bankruptcy court and then sold to repay your lenders. You may be able to keep some of your property under your state's exemptions. For example, in Ohio many of the exemptions have a specific dollar limit, such as work tools and equipment, which is limited to no more than $2,025. In other states, you may get a specific dollar amount, which all exempt property must fall into. Texas has a $60,000 exemption limit, so as long as the property you plan to keep is no more than $60,000 worth in total, you can keep it. Anything other than this must be returned to the lender or sold to repay your lenders.

For those who are filing Chapter 13 bankruptcy, the terms are somewhat different. Under this particular type of bankruptcy, you will not lose your assets. Rather, you get to keep them as long as your bankruptcy repayment plan allows for it. In this form of bankruptcy, all asset-based loans, or those loans that are secured by collateral, are repaid in full. However, these loans may be reorganized to make them easier for you to pay. In Chapter 13 bankruptcy, keep in mind that unsecured debt may be minimized or discharged depending on what that debt is. It is likely you purchased fuel and supplies with a credit card for your business;

this type of debt may be discharged in bankruptcy. Other types of debts, such as a loan used to buy valuable business equipment, may be reduced or may have to be repaid in full, depending on the rulings of the bankruptcy court. Again, if you have assets that can be liquidated to repay your debt, the bankruptcy court will do just that if you do not plan to repay what is owed on that debt.

In Chapter 13 bankruptcy, you can make a decision about what to keep and what to let go in some cases. You can determine if you want to keep paying on secured debts, for example. You may decide that some equipment can be let go to avoid having to repay that debt. For many businesses, secured debts such as real estate and equipment are necessary to keep the business operational. However, if you have two parcels of land for your business and only need one, you can turn over the second parcel to the lender you secured a loan from to buy that land. If this is done, any excess debt not repaid by the return of the property is forgiven during bankruptcy. If you purchased a parcel of land for $25,000 and you return it to your lender still owing $21,000 during a bankruptcy filing but the land is only worth $20,000 today, you are not held liable for that $1,000 loss.

You can only make decisions like this in regards to secured debt. In short, if you need it and want to keep it, you need to keep paying on it. If you do not want to keep paying on it, you can turn over the asset to the lender to settle the debt.

In LLCs and corporations, your private property is separated from your business property. In these cases, your personal property remains your own even if your business files bankruptcy.

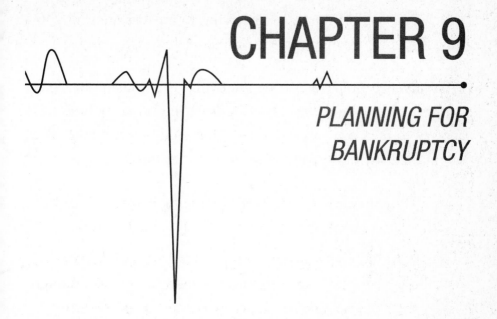

CHAPTER 9

PLANNING FOR BANKRUPTCY

Is your business ready to file bankruptcy? You have worked through your business's finances at this point. You have thought about your options and probably know which type of bankruptcy to file. However, keep in mind that you need to take some steps before you file to help protect yourself and your business moving forward.

As you plan for bankruptcy, there are several things you need to avoid doing and several things you can do to protect your hard-earned property. Many people make mistakes because they do not know better or may be trying to hide as much as they can from their creditors. However, one thing you absolutely need to realize is that if you try to hide something from your creditors or your bankruptcy trustee and it is later discovered, your entire bankruptcy case may be thrown out of court. What is worse is that your creditors may be able to garnish your wages or take your personal property as a way of being compensated for the debt you owe to them. Therefore, avoid any circumstances in which you could find yourself having to answer questions to a trustee about missing property or mistaken documents.

What some people do as they are facing the decision to file for bankruptcy for their business is look at the property they have and try to find ways to minimize what creditors can take. They might take any of the following steps, for example:

- They may try to hide assets by giving them away or by simply not listing them on bankruptcy paperwork.

- Some business owners will pay themselves bonuses or even try to start paying themselves a salary even though they had not taken a salary in the past. Having documentation of where money from the business has gone is critical.

- Some may pay off car loans or buy a new car using business funds.

- Some may try to pay off loans to some creditors or borrowers but not others.

- Some may simply take supplies, equipment, or other valuables from the business.

In all of these situations, you are positioning yourself for a ruling of abuse of bankruptcy filing. Let us take a closer look at how some of these situations can affect you should you decide to use them.

Hiding Your Assets

Hiding your assets ranges from simply giving property to family members to failing to report the property or other assets that you own. This is one of the most dangerous moves you can make as you prepare to file for bankruptcy because if discovered, you could face several punishments. These punishments may include discharge of your bankruptcy case and the requirement to pay all debts in full. The government sees this type of action as a way of defrauding the system. If, after an investigation, the government does find that you are hiding assets, such as uncovering them through an employee's statement or learning from some form of documentation, then this could amount to fraud charges in a court of law. It can land you in jail, too.

You may be wondering, how will they know? The government will find out about it in many cases simply because people tell the court. Your secretary might come forward or there might be coworkers who are less willing to allow you to defraud the system. If these individuals come forward to reveal you are hiding assets, this could lead to fraud charges. Further, your creditors know what you owe them and what you have purchased from them with borrowed funds. Because they know this information, they also know that you own the items. You may be asked to show proof you no longer own the item, such as producing a sales sheet that shows you sold it. If you never sold it, for example, you will not have this necessary proof. Further, if you had recently sold the item, that could be an example of trying to hide the asset itself.

Time to Take a Paycheck

When you start a small business and it grows, you begin to take a draw or even pay yourself a salary — this is how you will continue to pay your personal bills, after all. However, when the business starts to struggle, most business owners will stop or reduce the amount of money they take from the business. This is a way of providing the business with a bit more cash to make financial sense of the situation. This is normal, and there is nothing wrong with doing this. Business owners want their businesses to have everything necessary to succeed. However, there does become a problem when a small-business owner starts to consider taking a draw or a salary after not doing so once the business becomes insolvent. In other words, if you are not taking a paycheck right now and your business is struggling to the point of considering bankruptcy, taking a paycheck now could be seen as a way of defrauding the government.

You may see those extra funds in the accounts and you may think that you can easily justify paying yourself again for your hard work, but that is not the way that the courts will see it. If your corporation files Chapter 7 bankruptcy, the U.S. trustee carefully scrutinizes all of those assets in corporate accounts. The court may make you pay back those funds because to them, it seems to be evidence of fraud. The courts see you, the business owner, as a creditor in this case. The business does owe you money for the work you put into it, but if other creditors are not being paid as the agreements state they would be, then you should not be paid either. It is similar to showing favoritism to one creditor over another. Business owners who try to do this will go to jail for doing so in many cases.

What if you own a sole proprietorship? In this situation, you are not doing yourself any favors. Because all of your personal and business debts are considered the same when you file for bankruptcy, you will end up having to pay creditors back those funds.

Car Payments

Once you start looking at the details of bankruptcy, you may notice that you are able to keep a car under most state exemptions. However, before you buy yourself a new one or you start to pay off your current car loan, realize that there are some stipulations.

If you have an asset, such as a car, that has plenty of built-up equity, that value may be used to pay down your debts during bankruptcy. For example, if your state exemptions say that you can own a car with no more equity than $4,000, and your car is worth more, it might be necessary to sell the car to withdraw the equity from it to pay down creditors.

Consider this scenario: You decide to pay off your $5,000 car so that you can keep the car after your debts are clear. You find out that the state's exemption is only $4,000 for one vehicle, and the value of the car is $5,000 currently. This gives you two options once you file for bankruptcy: You can give the car back and receive back money that is equal to the exemption limit in your state when the car is sold, or you have to pay the difference. In this situation, you are not only paying for the car the first time around, but you are paying for it a second time to the trustee in order to keep the vehicle.

However, you can avoid this. If you allow the loan to remain in good standing, you can continue to make payments on the vehicle. Sticking with the same example, if you still owe $3,000 on the car loan and the vehicle is worth $5,000, the actual equity in the vehicle is $2,000. That is below the state's exemption level, and therefore you can keep the vehicle if you agree to continue making payments. Keep in mind that if you do not want to own the car anymore and do not want to make payments, you can give this asset back to the lender.

What about buying a new car, then: This is also not a good option for most people. First off, if you take money from your business to buy a new car, you create the same situation as listed above. You will either have to allow the bankruptcy court to sell the vehicle if it is over the state's exemptions, or you will have to come up with the difference between the value of the car and the state's exemptions. Also, if you purchase the vehicle too close to filing for bankruptcy, the courts may see this as a way of defrauding the court. The courts will look into your accounts over the last six months to determine if you have made any significant payments or purchases that could be an indication of fraud, such as those more than $600. Do not purchase any new assets if you plan to file for bankruptcy.

If you need a new car or you are concerned about your car and how it will be affected during the bankruptcy, contact your attorney to see what your options are and how to handle your specific situation.

Paying Off Loans

It may seem like a good idea to pay off one lender before you file for bankruptcy. This, too, is a mistake. It is especially problematic if you are paying off loans to family members and to friends first, even if they are investors in your business and you borrowed money from them to start or fund your business.

Payments made to family members are specifically listed as unallowable under bankruptcy code. They are considered insiders. Payments to insiders, even over the last two years prior to filing, amounts to an illegal action and the courts can require that the funds be returned. This is called recapturing the funds. Some business owners may feel as if paying off a family loan with what is left over will simply settle a debt, but in the eyes of the bankruptcy court it is a type of fraud.

What makes this process even more problematic is that if you have been making payments on your family-funded loan consistently over the last months, the bankruptcy trustee can require that those funds be recaptured and equally distributed to your creditors. For example, you may have borrowed $15,000 from a friend to start your business. Each month, you pay your friend $500 toward what you borrowed. You have been doing the same thing for the last two years and have paid the friend back a total of $12,000 in that timeframe. The problem is, this person is a close friend and the courts can require that all $12,000 worth of those payments be recaptured by the courts and distributed to creditors equally. In many instances, and as terrible as it seems, your friend may not have the funds to repay to the trustee and may be required to repay the funds over time or file for bankruptcy himself or herself. Often, you may go to family friends with equity in their home or you may encourage them to allow you to borrow against their retirement plan. In effect, they do not have the funds to turn over to the trustee, but they may be held liable to do just that.

Although it may be too late to make changes now, keep in mind that borrowing from family and close friends is almost never a good idea when it comes to funding business transactions because of instances like the above circumstance. For some people, this situation may be one of the main reasons not to file for bankruptcy if it can be avoided in any way.

Taking Supplies from the Business

Just like taking money out of business accounts, you can get yourself in trouble by taking business assets or supplies within the six months prior to filing for bankruptcy. Some people think that they can take the equipment and hide it away in their garage and later start a new business using it, for example. Alternatively, you may want to hide some of the supplies you have to sell online after the bankruptcy has gone through. Like with other circumstances listed here, if the bankruptcy courts find out about this transaction, you could face fraud charges. This type of action often occurs with smaller items, such as laptops or other electronics that are easy to hide and do not have a title that follows them from place to place. Even the software you purchase to manage your business should be included in your bankruptcy documentation to avoid it being considered a hidden asset.

Any time you take anything from the business that was purchased with business funds or a business line of credit and then file for bankruptcy, you are committing bankruptcy fraud. Avoid doing this at all costs to avoid any criminal action brought against you. If you have any questions about the title or the ownership of property, consult with your attorney before making any decisions to specifically not include items.

What happens if you discover assets later on? If the assets could have been missed, such as not accounting for an unused piece of equipment, then the bankruptcy trustee will allow you to add this to your bankruptcy case in most instances without recourse. Do so as soon as possible, though there is no specific timeframe or restriction in place. You will need to show the debt or assets were purchased prior to filing for bankruptcy. It is always better for you to present such forgotten assets rather than to allow the courts to discover them on their own. Be honest about any mistakes you make in your documentation to avoid any type of repercussions.

Hire an Attorney

So far, we have covered many of the mistakes you can make when you are preparing to file for bankruptcy, but it is also important for you to further your plans. Specifically, you need to hire an attorney.

Hiring an attorney is an important step you will need to take. You can contact an attorney local to you that you have worked with in the past. You can obtain a recommendation from someone you know. You can look in a phone book, too. However, there are a few things to keep in mind before hiring just anyone.

Choose an attorney based on his or her experience in the type of bankruptcy you plan to file. You also can ask for references and ask about their track record of successes in filing bankruptcies. It is always a good idea to sit down with the attorney for an interview. This one-on-one interview allows you to ask questions and to learn what the attorney's advice is. Further, you will be able to judge if you can trust the attorney with your business. You may even want to talk to several attorneys before making a decision on just one.

The reason for hiring an attorney is simple. Business bankruptcy is more intense, and it often requires you to deal with more types of creditors, including contractors you want to keep working with. If you plan to keep you business operational, for example, you need to work with creditors who you owe money to but still need to do business with. This is a situation that a bankruptcy attorney can help you with. It is also very important for you to take into consideration the various facets of your business, such as:

- Do you have employees that you owe money to?

- Do you owe money to the government, such as past taxes?

- Do you have creditors who are threatening to repossess assets right now?

- Are you unable to separate your business income from your private income and assets?

- Are you struggling with payments to agencies such as workers' compensation, your liability insurance, or to business organizations?

These are just some of the complex situations you need to deal with when it comes to filing for bankruptcy as a business. Each situation may be unique, and each of those specific situations may require a different solution. The dissolving of a business takes more steps and more effort than filing for bankruptcy personally. For this reason, and because there are more people involved in business bankruptcy, it is a good idea to hire an attorney to handle your business bankruptcy case for you.

First off, the bankruptcy attorney can help you avoid bankruptcy in some situations. If you choose an attorney who has the means to work with creditors and work out debt repayment plans, this could allow you to have a professional by your side to help you to work through your debt and avoid having to file for bankruptcy. You also get their professional opinion on if this is an option for you and your business or if it is simply a better option to file for bankruptcy. Look for a settlement attorney for this.

Here are a few of the additional benefits you may have by investing in an attorney:

- Your attorney can help you to define your liability in the business debt. For example, the attorney can help determine what type of business status you hold legally and what that means for your business and personal debt. Although this book does that for you, you may have unique circumstances or further questions.

- A bankruptcy attorney can help you to work through the means test and other qualifications that are part of the bankruptcy process. These are covered in Chapter 10 to some degree, but you will still benefit from having an attorney work through the process for you.

- An attorney will ensure that you meet all requirements of the bankruptcy court, which ranges from the order the bankruptcy documents are placed to the timeline you need to follow to submit all documents.

- An attorney can help you to uncover all assets and expenses to form a Chapter 13 repayment plan, which will help you to work through the bankruptcy process. A repayment plan is something that you need to draft with the aid and approval of your trustee otherwise.

- The bankruptcy attorney can also help you manage your business during bankruptcy. If your business needs to purchase equipment or needs to make other larger transactions, approval from the courts is necessary, but you do need to show the necessity of such payments properly.

There is value in hiring an attorney to handle your business bankruptcy. However, you may be wondering what to expect when you do hire this type of professional to manage your bankruptcy case.

There are several things to look for in a bankruptcy attorney, depending on what type of business you have. Some attorneys specialize in helping only those who have personal bankruptcy filings or those who have sole proprietorships — these two are often lumped together because they are virtually the same in legal bankruptcy terms. Some attorneys specialize in providing services to those who have corporations or LLCs. Other attorneys provide service to anyone filing for bankruptcy.

If the attorney has a specialization, this means that he or she has better insight and experience in that type of bankruptcy. In addition, you want to look for an attorney who has a solid reputation as being a quality service provider. You can find a great deal of information about the attorney by asking for referrals or even calling the local board to learn more about his or her past experiences and complaints.

Once you find an attorney, it is time to tell him or her what your needs are. You need to interview him or her to learn if the attorney is the right person for the job by looking for the following:

- Learn if the attorney provides services in cases like yours. This is especially important if you have any type of specialized circumstance, such as a business that you want out of that your partner does not want to shutter. In this case, a legal agreement between the two parties is necessary and should be formed with the aid of an attorney.

- Inform the attorney about your particular concerns. Does the attorney respond to you and answer your questions? During a consultation, it is appropriate for the attorney to use hypothetical examples and information, especially because most of these meetings are actually free consultations. Still, you should walk away having answers to most of your questions.

- Provide information to the attorney about any circumstances you are interested in particularly. For example, if you are not sure what type of bankruptcy is best for you, it is always best to get an attorney's opinion.

- Learn about all attorney fees prior to determining whether you will work with the attorney. This is critical because it can be expensive to hire an attorney for most types of business bankruptcy cases, simply because there is additional work for the attorney to do.

Locating a great attorney only makes your job easier. However, it is not always necessary for you to hire an attorney, especially if you are filing for bankruptcy as a sole proprietor. But as you will see in the next chapters, the process of filing for bankruptcy is multistep and that means making key decisions that will affect your personal and business finances for the long term.

Common Myths About Bankruptcy

Before working through bankruptcy decisions and filing methods, it is first important to dispel a few myths. One myth is that filing for bankruptcy is too embarrassing or is an admittance of failure. The stigma of bankruptcy simply no longer fits. With the financial crisis occurring in 2008 through 2010, it has become more common for individuals to file for bankruptcy. However, that does not mean that taking filing for bankruptcy lightly is a good thing. You want to invest careful planning so that you can avoid it going forward. Consider the following myths about bankruptcy; you may find that the process is not a bad fit for your particular needs. Realize that your financial situation can improve with the right steps, of which bankruptcy may be one.

Myth No.1: "My credit will be ruined."

It is likely that filing for bankruptcy will damage your credit, which means it will be more difficult to start a business afterward. Lenders will be less likely to extend credit to you because you have demonstrated poor previous financial management skill. This is a factor you need to keep in mind when filing for bankruptcy.

Why is it a myth? Though it is possible for small business owners with good credit to file for bankruptcy, it is more common that those who file will already have damaged credit. Many people spend a great deal of time trying to work through debt repayment on their own, trying to find a solution to pay down the debt they owe. However, over time, this process really does wear down your credit, and it can lead to a significantly poor credit score, especially if you have stopped making payments on your loans or you have becoming behind on your mortgage.

Bankruptcy will hurt your credit, but not filing for bankruptcy could extend your financial problems even longer, including lowering your credit score. You could find yourself facing creditor calls, foreclosures, and even repossessions of your business equipment or personal belongings if you do not file. For most who are considering bankruptcy because they have tried everything else, bankruptcy can be the start of improving your credit. Once you file, the debts are wiped out or restructured. You get a fresh start.

Myth No. 2: "Everyone will know."

No one likes his or her financial business to be front page of the local newspaper, but it is important to realize that it most likely will not. Small businesses filing for bankruptcy could be included in the newspaper, but it is unlikely that this will happen unless your business is a prominent one in the city.

However, it is possible for people to learn about your bankruptcy. In fact, it is a matter of public record. That does not mean, however, that this is going to be something people will do.

Why is this a myth then? Though it is possible that your business bankruptcy case will be made known, most small businesses will not be exposed in a way that will hurt their business. In fact, it is likely that only those you tell will learn of your bankruptcy. This should not be a reason that you fail to file if you need to. Further, the fact that you could see your business fail completely if you do not file, which might be front-page news, is a reason to consider bankruptcy.

Myth No. 3: "It will affect my spouse's credit."

If you file for bankruptcy as a small-business owner, your personal finances, including your assets and sometimes your debts, will play a role in what occurs with your business debts. For example, if you own a sole proprietorship, filing Chapter 7 bankruptcy will include any debt that you are listed on, and all of your personal assets will be part of that debt filing. However, it is also important to note that unless you include your spouse on your business or on your business debt, he or she is protected from the effects of the bankruptcy.

If you both own a credit card and that credit card becomes part of the bankruptcy filing, the creditor may try to come after your spouse for payment in full. Because your spouse is listed on the account, he or she is liable. If this is the case with most of your debt, you may want to have your spouse file for bankruptcy at the same time. However, if this is not the case and most of your bankruptcy includes debt that is in your name only, it may not be necessary for your spouse to be involved yet.

Your spouse's credit remains intact as long as all of his or her debts are being paid on time and are separate from your business debt. However, if you own assets together, do keep in mind that some of those assets may be liquidated in the bankruptcy. Therefore, your spouse may end up losing assets that are not otherwise protected, such as through exemptions. It is important to talk to your spouse about the potential effects of bankruptcy for your small business on his or her assets before you file.

It is also important for you to check credit reports after you file for bankruptcy and your debts are discharged. Ensure that your spouse checks his or her credit report as well. To check a credit report from the three major credit bureaus, visit **www.annualcreditreport.com** and follow the provided steps. Sometimes, though rarely, it is possible for a notation to be entered onto the spouse's credit report by a creditor stating that the debt was discharged through bankruptcy. If your spouse did not sign on to the debt originally and therefore is not responsible for the debt, he or she can file a complaint with the credit bureau and the notation will be removed from his or her credit report.

Myth No. 4: "I will lose everything."

For those who are struggling with the decision to file for bankruptcy for your business because your personal assets and debts are subject to the bankruptcy court's decision, there should be concern about losing everything.

First off, if you are filing Chapter 13 bankruptcy, you will not lose your assets unless you decide to lose them, such as giving back an asset to settle a debt. If you are filing Chapter 7 as a sole proprietor, you should be more concerned about the types of property you will lose. However, you will not lose everything. In fact, it is likely that your home and vehicles will be protected throughout the bankruptcy. Any assets related to your business will be sold by the bankruptcy trustee to repay your debts. However, when it comes to personal assets, the bankruptcy trustee is unable to take any property that falls under your state's exemptions.

State exemptions protect homes and cars up to a certain value or with a specific amount of equity, and the amount of these allowances differs from state to state. It makes sense that if you have a home filled with luxurious and expensive items that the bankruptcy court is likely to sell those items to repay your lenders. After all, you are defaulting on a debt you agreed to take on. If you have assets that are worth selling and that are in fact not protected by exemptions, you may lose them. The bankruptcy court will take possession of those assets and will sell them or turn them over to the lender. However, there will not likely be a large auction in front of your home, as some people believe from watching movies. Even if you lose your home, it is unlikely that you will have such an auction. Rather, these properties are often sold through a county auction house.

Myth No. 5: "I will lose my job and license."

It is highly unlikely that you will lose your job just because you filed bankruptcy. If your employer terminates your employment for no other reason than because you file for bankruptcy, you could file a lawsuit against the employer because law prohibits this. Again, your employer is not likely to know about your bankruptcy unless you inform them of it.

However, this is not as clear-cut when it comes to any licenses that you have. In most situations, you will not lose your license to perform tasks unless the agency has a specific rule about bankruptcy filing. For example, you are not going to lose your driver's license because you filed for bankruptcy. If you have a state or local established license to do business in the area, there may be stipulations on bankruptcy filings. For example, in some types of insurance and financial industries, filing for bankruptcy may be something that requires you to get a new license or to demonstrate your business's financial stability before you start collecting money from your clients. You will need to check with the licensing authority in the state to find out if this is the case for your particular license. Look to the Web site of the licensing authority or use your license documentation to find this organization. In most cases, it is not something that occurs.

Myth No. 6: "I will not recover from this."

Bankruptcy is a last act; it is a method of getting your debts under control, but it is not the final act. In other words, it is a fresh start to give you a chance to make better financial decisions from here on out. Although it will have a tremendous effect on your overall financial state for quite a while, such as limiting the availability to loans you have, it is not going to stop you from living a relatively normal lifestyle because:

- You will still be able to hold a bank account.

- You will be able to maintain your retirement accounts and savings accounts for your future.

- You will be able to get student loans again, though it may be difficult to do so right after your bankruptcy is discharged.

- You will be able to get credit again. In fact, you are likely to start receiving offers for limited lines of credit within six months to two years of your bankruptcy being discharged. This is an opportunity to slowly rebuild your credit score. It can take years to rebuild your credit score, and every person will have a different timeframe depending on how you use credit in the future.

It will take time to recover from your bankruptcy. However, not filing for bankruptcy could potentially hurt you, especially if you continue to fall behind on your debts. *Chapter 11 of this book provides you with some resources and tips to help you to build a stronger financial future after you have filed bankruptcy.* You can overcome this debt problem and get that fresh start.

Myth No. 7: "I will go to jail if I do not pay my bills."

A century or more ago, laws in many local jurisdictions allowed creditors to put those who did not pay their debts into jail. The good news is that this is not the way things are in modern times. Today, bankruptcies and debt nonpayment is not a matter for the criminal courts. It is a civil matter and because of that, the government has no way of putting you in jail for not paying your debts back, even if you file for bankruptcy. According to the law, once you field bankruptcy and the bankruptcy court discharges your debts, no creditor can come after you in any way for those debts. In fact, if they do so, they could be fined considerably.

Finally, although there is still some stigma attached to filing for bankruptcy, most of that stigma is self-made. You are more likely to be hard on yourself when it comes to filing for bankruptcy rather than other people. This is especially true for businesses because the rate of failure for a business is so high. Taking the time to work through any of these concerns is something that you need to do before you file. Having an attorney by your side through the process will help you to avoid any potential problems or concerns that are still lingering.

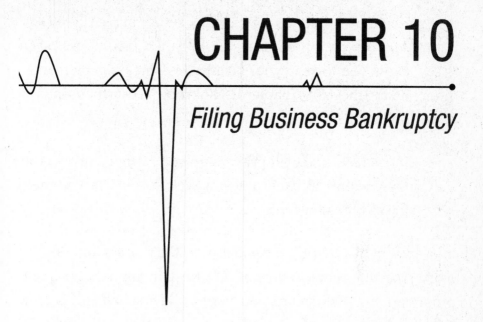

CHAPTER 10

Filing Business Bankruptcy

Now that you have gotten to the point of understanding your bankruptcy options and how it will fit your business, it is time to file for bankruptcy. As a small-business owner, you need to keep the following in mind:

- If you have a sole proprietorship or a partnership and you want to get rid of all of your debts, you will need to file Chapter 7 bankruptcy. In doing so, your personal and business-related debts are viewed the same.

- If you business is a corporation or an LLC, you have the option of filing Chapter 7 bankruptcy. However, your business will need to close its doors, as the trustee will liquidate its assets to repay debt. Corporations cannot receive a full discharge of unpaid debt under bankruptcy code.

- If you own a corporation or LLC, you can file Chapter 11 bankruptcy, but not Chapter 13 bankruptcy. These plans allow you to keep your business's doors open by reorganizing the debt. Chapter 11 bankruptcy costs thousands of dollars to file.

- If you have a sole proprietorship or a partnership, you can file Chapter 13 bankruptcy as well, as long as you meet the requirements.

In the rest of this chapter, we will outline the process for filing for bankruptcy for a corporation or LLC. Keep in mind that as a sole proprietor or a partnership, you can use the first half of this book to file for bankruptcy, because there is no difference in your business and personal debts.

Filing for Chapter 7

Filing for Chapter 7 bankruptcy is the best way to close your business's doors. As mentioned earlier, your business can use this type of bankruptcy, but you will need to sell off all of your assets to do so, which means there is no way for your business to continue to operate. Further, if you own a corporation or an LLC, you could remain responsible for some debts after your business files bankruptcy. The debts of these types of businesses are not discharged in full; however, they are often minimized and are repaid through assets in most cases.

What happens in this form of bankruptcy? The first step is to take the means test by filling out the Statement of Current Monthly Income and Means Test Calculations. This document is available through your attorney or through the bankruptcy court. This document asks you questions about your income as well as your expenses. The goal of it is to determine if your leftover profit is enough to pay creditors based on your income and your setoffs, or expenses. The means test used for small businesses is a bit more complex than what is used for personal bankruptcy cases. This is one of those instances when those organized financial records will be very helpful to you.

Once you pass the means test, you can move forward with your bankruptcy. *Chapter 3 of this book contains a full explanation of how to pass a means test.* The next step is to complete consumer credit counseling, which is a type of credit management program you will need to enroll in and try out before filing for bankruptcy. You will need a certificate from this organization showing that you completed the program and attempted the process.

You will also need to take a financial management course after you file for bankruptcy. This course also provides you with a certificate that shows you have taken the course. The course teaches you how to manage financials better so that you can better avoid filing for bankruptcy again. The bankruptcy court provides specific organizations for this purpose, and many consumer debt-counseling agencies provide these services as well.

If you have any debts that you plan to keep, you will need to file a form called Reaffirmation Agreements with each of those lenders. For example, if you have a car loan, but you wish to keep the loan and keep making full payments on it, you will need to file this form with the courts to reestablish your agreement to pay the debt as initially outlined.

The next steps in the process remain the same as personal bankruptcy filing. *You can find more information in Chapter 3, 4 and 5 of this book.* You will need to fill out a stack of documents that list your debts and your real and personal property, and you will need to list all of the contracts, leases, and other financial resources you have. All of this information, including business income and expenses are organized through "schedules," which is another term for a form. These documents will be submitted to the bankruptcy court once complete.

Once the documents are filed

As we have mentioned, it is best to have your bankruptcy forms submitted to the bankruptcy court (and your case managed by) an attorney. He or she will have the ability and the means to help you in the filing process and ensure each detail is maintained as the court requires, such as ensuring all documentation is accurately filled out. Attorneys can also provide you with more guidance on your unique case. Once those documents have been submitted to the bankruptcy court in your county, something called an automatic stay is put in place. Then, creditors can no longer contact you, try to collect from you, or continue legal action against your debts. Foreclosures are put on hold at this point.

The person who handles your case once it has been filed is called your trustee. The trustee is not working for you, but rather is working on behalf of the creditors. His or her job is to get as much money from you as is possible to pay back to the creditors. The trustee is generally someone that you want to show respect for, because they can decide to dig further into your case if they would like to. Do as he or she asks to ensure the process goes smoothly. The trustee rarely needs to contact you other than for clarification about documents or information if it was not presented properly or thoroughly the first time. The trustee will look through the case and will make determinations about whether your bankruptcy should go through, based on the information that is provided to you. The trustee can send the case back for clarification or stop it. The trustee can also convert it to another form of bankruptcy, such as changing from a Chapter 7 to a Chapter 13.

The only time when you are likely to come into contact with your creditors is during a 341 meeting. This meeting is a short interview with you that is audio recorded and sometimes video recorded. You will need to answer questions about the debt, such as how it was accumulated and why you cannot repay it. They will ask you how the debt was accumulated. They will also ask what type of financial hardships brought on the debt. Each trustee is different, but most just want you to state why you are in this position. This is known as a meeting of creditors. Though the creditors are informed of the meeting and allowed to attend, this very rarely happens unless your business has a great deal of assets. You do not need to worry about creditors. Even if they are present, only a statement is taken from them.

Creditors may come to this meeting if they feel that you were dishonest in your application to them for credit. Although they may have little recourse in getting you to repay the debt, they can ask questions and they can argue that you are abusing the bankruptcy process in some way, such as you are not being honest about your assets. The trustee is then obligated to investigate any claims made by the creditors to ensure that your documents are accurate. It is unlikely that they will attend, though, because most Chapter 7 bankruptcy filings have few assets for liquidation and therefore there is nothing for creditors to get from you. You will have no assets to liquidate for repayment of the debt.

After your 341 meeting

In most cases, once you have gone through the 341 meeting, you will spend the next few weeks waiting. It can take several weeks for the bankruptcy trustee to work through your case and after that point, unless your creditors have challenged the bankruptcy case, you will likely be waiting for your discharge documents to arrive. It is important to note that if the creditors do challenge the bankruptcy, you may be required to verify your debt and assets by providing further documentation. Further questions may be asked of you to verify the claims you have made on your documentation. As long as your documents are thorough and accurate, you should not have a problem. Though questions are rare, it is important to be thorough and honest on your bankruptcy documentation to ensure that these questions are easily answered. Some common problems that may arise on the filing of bankruptcy include:

- Giving your family property.

- Inheritances.

- Tax refunds (the bankruptcy court can collect these to use to repay your lenders).

- Missing property (you forgot or you intentionally did not list something).

Unless there is some reason to believe that you are abusing the system, your debt will be discharged once all information is provided and is verified by the courts. If the bankruptcy trustee does believe that your case is abusive, he or she may reject the bankruptcy petition. It can take three to five months to learn about your discharge. The difference in time in this case is based on how fast your bankruptcy court can work through the paperwork.

Filing Chapter 11 or Chapter 13

Unless you plan to close your business, Chapter 11 and Chapter 13 are the routes to take. The goal of these types of bankruptcy is to stop the financial disaster that continues to surround your business. This type of bankruptcy does not guarantee that the business will remain open. Rather, this type of bankruptcy allows the facts to be taken into consideration, including:

- Can the business operate successfully even if it means considerably stripping the business down and reducing debt?

- Is it a better option for the business to liquidate its assets and exit the business in an orderly manner?

The answers to those questions come only after the business works through the documents. In many cases, your bankruptcy attorney will be able to give you some direction on which route is most likely to occur for your business. Otherwise, you will need to make this decision for yourself.

Chapter 11

In most situations, this particular type of bankruptcy deals with the fact that when most business assets are sold, they are unlikely enough to cover all of the debt the business has. Most of the equipment sold from a business, for example, is so specialized and functions solely for that business that it is worth little to any other business owner and therefore it does not usually fetch a good price when sold. Also, used equipment is often far less valuable than new equipment. It is often, therefore, hard for the trustee to find a business to purchase them. Further, when a business closes its doors, this affects not only the business itself and its owners but also all of the stakeholders in that business, which includes customers, employees, and investors. If the business can be kept intact, even through bankruptcy, it may be the best route for all involved in that business. The trustee knows this and is likely to try to keep a potentially profitable business open.

Speaking specifically of Chapter 11, this type of bankruptcy may sometimes be used to help avoid the bad contracts that a business has taken on that have become too difficult or financially draining for the business to hold on to and turn a profit. For example, the business may need to get out of a lease on a property that is performing poorly, such as a satellite of the company that does not have customers, or it may need to break a contract with a vendor. This type of bankruptcy can help to break those contracts, too, by rewriting the terms of the contract.

Another way to use Chapter 11 bankruptcy is to help dispose of the business piece by piece while determining which creditors receive the cash generated. If the business owner wishes to sell some of the business assets or even the business as an ongoing operation, this type of bankruptcy can help that process to occur by legally organizing creditors for payment and relinquishing the business from contracts. The Chapter 11 bankruptcy gives the seller and the buyer protection over any creditor who may wish to come after the business and seize property or assets.

The process of filing Chapter 11 bankruptcy is similar to that of any other bankruptcy in that you need to file a petition with the courts outlining your desire to file. By doing this, the business or the individual, depending on who is filing the bankruptcy, is immediately protected by the bankruptcy courts from creditors and foreclosure proceedings. At this time, the bankruptcy courts technically own and run the business. However, most business owners will file documents that allow the business to be run as debtor possession, meaning that the court owns the business but the debtor is running the business. This is a formality. In most cases, the court will want to maintain ownership, because the business ownership and management are most likely to know the business well enough to run it.

Though the court has this type of ownership, it will require some specific documents and legal reports to be created, maintained, and presented. You will need to provide a running account of what is being done within the business and how assets are being disposed of specifically. Each month, the court will require you to file a report that will outline the assets being used within the business. This is one of the more difficult tasks for a small-business owner because it is time-consuming and often is not a simple or straightforward process. If your business has significant monthly revenue, such as more than $10,000 a month, or has more than 50 employees, hire an attorney to help you through this process or use an accountant familiar with the process. The financial strain of an attorney or accountant can make an already strapped small business struggle even more.

Another aspect of Chapter 11 bankruptcy is the formation of the committee of creditors. The committee of creditors is established by the U.S. trustee assigned to the case and is made up of the creditors with the seven largest unsecured claims against the debtor. In a larger corporation where the business has numerous lenders and debts, having a smaller group or committee of creditors who will speak for and legally represent all of the creditors the business has makes sense, and it may even simplify the process. However, for a small business, this is limiting because most small businesses already only have a handful of creditors. The meeting of creditors is an opportunity for the business owner to explain the situation he or she is in to the creditors. What happened? Why is the business struggling? The creditors will also question the business owner to determine what the actual situation is.

The next step in the Chapter 11 bankruptcy is the independent reporting. A third-party organization is appointed to investigate the business, usually an accountant or lawyer-based firm chosen by the trustee. It will give a full report on the problems within the business and the prospects for the business after working through financial documents you provide. You will need to pay the fees for this third-party organization, which vary depending on the extent of time required to investigate the business.

Once all of this is complete, a disclosure statement is sent to the court for approval, outlining the standing of the business in terms of assets and debt. It gives a clear summary of the plan of reorganization to the court and the types of creditors the business has. It defines how these creditors will be treated. The statement also presents the alternatives if the bankruptcy is not forthcoming, such as complete liquidation. The U.S. trustee will hold a hearing to present these options to all involved parties, including creditors and debtors.

The plan of reorganization needs to be completed before the disclosure statement is sent to the courts, because this plan is what the court needs to decide upon. It details how every class of creditor will be treated in the bankruptcy. The term "class" here is used to describe one or more creditors who share a similar situation with other creditors, such as the amount owed and the type of debt owed. For example, secured creditors are different from unsecured creditors. This information determines the importance of the creditor, based on what is owed to them.

The classification of creditors is one of the more complex aspects of Chapter 11 bankruptcy. How each one is classified will ultimately determine how these creditors will vote, such as for the reorganization plan or against it. When a vote is conducted of the class of creditors, it is based on majority rules. Therefore, this classification of creditors is critical to the business because it positions the business better for a majority vote in favor of the business. For example, if the business hopes to utilize reorganization that minimizes unsecured debts or eliminates them, if those creditors are classified as least important, this works to the advantage of the business. This organization is done with your attorney and trustee and is approved by the creditors.

It is critical that the reorganization plan of the business be put together in an effective manner to achieve this type of balance, so that the end result is what the business owner needs and wants. The organization plan takes into consideration the classification of the creditors. If the small business owner notices that one classification of creditor does not approve of a specific provision within the plan, the plan may be altered to better accommodate that class. The business owner and his or her attorney will negotiate with the creditors about the treatment of the creditor's classification. While every creditor wants to be paid in full of what is owed to them, by showing what the alternatives are — such as making payment in full of the debt over a longer period of time in lieu of discharging that debt — the attorney can help negotiate with the creditor. The goal here is to get every creditor to agree that the reorganization plan in place is the best option for all involved. Accepting something is better than the alternative, for example, which is often liquidation of the business.

This process goes back and forth until the majority accepts an agreement. The attorney presents the reorganization plan to the creditors. The creditors who think they can get more from the case may vote against the plan, which sends it back to the attorney. Creditors do this to try and get better terms in their favor. The plan has to keep in mind, though, that the business owner needs some consolidations if it is to remain open and functioning. If there is an unrealistic plan provision, such as making a payment that is too large for the business to afford, this may kill the business in itself. This back-and-forth movement continues until all agree on the plan in place.

As you can see, this complex process of filing Chapter 11 nearly always requires the use of an attorney to handle the classification of creditors and negotiations of a reorganization plan. This is one of the main reasons that the cost of Chapter 11 is much higher than other forms of bankruptcy. However, Chapter 11 is not the only option for some business owners.

Chapter 13

Chapter 13 bankruptcy is the combination of Chapter 7 and Chapter 11 bankruptcies, and it can be a faster, simpler process for those business owners who select this method. However, only sole proprietors and partnerships may file Chapter 13. All types of bankruptcy are complex, but what Chapter 13 does for a business is simplify the overall process, requiring less hands-on administration from the bankruptcy trustee and creditors.

A Chapter 13 bankruptcy is a good option for any business hoping to remain intact after the bankruptcy because unlike that of a Chapter 7 bankruptcy, this form allows you to keep all of your assets and helps to reorganize the debt to make it easier for you to repay. Small-business owners are able to repay their debts, which for some is a moral obligation they want to keep; they just need some help getting to that point. Chapter 13 provides that help.

A Chapter 13 bankruptcy is stretched out over three to five years, depending on the length of time you would need to repay your debts. Keep in mind that you will go through many of the same steps in this form of bankruptcy as you would in Chapter 7 bankruptcy in terms of the types of documents you will submit and the qualifications for the means test. However, there are some differences to become familiar with:

- A means test is still conducted, but now the means test is more about determining the size of the debt that needs to be repaid and the term that it will be repaid in. This is called the Statement of Current Monthly Income and Calculations of Commitment Period and Disposable Income.

- The method of determining income is complex, and it requires understanding some of the most commonly changing bankruptcy laws and regulations. Further, business expenses must be determined first, and then funds are set aside for payment of those expenses. Because you have a business, your income calculations will focus on business expenses as well as personal expenses, because you are filing for personal bankruptcy as well.

- You will need to work through credit-counseling services. These organizations look at your ability to avoid bankruptcy and to continue to repay your debt in a traditional manner. Once you have a meeting with such an organization, you will obtain a certificate of credit counseling that needs to be submitted with your bankruptcy documents when you file.

The documentation for a Chapter 13 bankruptcy is similar to that of a Chapter 7, which was discussed earlier. It has a proposed plan of how debts will be repaid, and it has a statement of financial affairs. This is the most important element of any Chapter 13 bankruptcy. When comparing this plan to that of one included in the Chapter 11 bankruptcy plan, the biggest difference is simplicity. This plan outlines how each of the creditor classes will be paid. As a small business, you do not need to submit to the scrutiny and the details that a larger corporation would.

The plan outlines the length of the proposed repayment, how much each creditor will receive, and how much the attorney representing you will be paid for his or her services. In most cases, secured creditors are paid in full or partially paid, depending on the agreement with the bankruptcy court. Unsecured creditors are generally repaid partially, but a business owner can elect to repay all of his or her debts in full, choose which of the unsecured debts to pay, or repay in full through the plan. For example, if you have a cosigner on the loan with you, you may want to pay the loan in full to protect the cosigner. If you wish to keep a creditor, paying them in full may be necessary.

You need to focus on two elements when it comes to constructing an effective plan. Any unsecured lender, such as a credit card lender or personal loan lender, must receive at least what he or she would have received under a Chapter 7 bankruptcy through the plan. In addition, the business owner must devote all of his or her disposable income to the repayment plan. Disposable income is the money that is left over after all of the expenses are paid — all reasonable living expenses must be paid first. However, this second element can cause a problem for some small-business owners. In particular, if the creditors do not believe that the disposable income reported in the plan is actual, they can object to it, which would open a hearing and further scrutiny to determine if in fact the information is accurate. If the creditor believes you are hiding assets, for example, this could open a hearing. There are some areas where creditors commonly consider reasonable living expenses problematic, including:

- The cost of food

- Entertainment costs listed

- Private schooling for children

- Repayment of loans against retirement plans

• Charitable giving

If you have these types of elements listed in your repayment plan as a part of your living expenses, creditors may object. That does not mean you should not include them, but it does mean that they need to be accurate and important, such as paying for entertainment costs to secure a business deal. The proposed plan will also include information on which creditors will be repaid fully. It will list any property that the small business will surrender as part of the plan if this is likely to happen. It will also list any contracts or leases that will be kept or given up.

Once you have completed the proposed plan — with an attorney's help, if possible — you will then submit it to the bankruptcy court. Like with a Chapter 7 bankruptcy, you will need to then wait for the bankruptcy trustee to schedule the first meeting of creditors. At this meeting, creditors can question you regarding the debts, and creditors can object to the proposed plan you have submitted. If there is an objection, the trustee will listen to it and determine if further inquiry is necessary. Objections are handled by the trustee, not you. The creditors are notified to file claims and verify how much they are owed. Assuming there is no objection, the plan goes into effect. If there is an objection, a hearing is scheduled where all involved attend to work through the circumstances.

Once the plan is in place, you will spend the next three to five years repaying the debts. Unlike the Chapter 7 bankruptcy, you will remain in control of your assets throughout the Chapter 13 plan, but you legally are working under a debtor in possession of bankruptcy property — or simply a debtor in possession — clause, which means you are accountable to the courts for the use of any of your assets during the repayment period. You need to be ready to account for the property at any time that the court says you must.

What does that mean? Here are a few scenarios to keep in mind:

- Property that you have included in the bankruptcy estate cannot be sold immediately. It is important to note that the property belongs to the bankruptcy estate throughout the time you are in this position. You cannot just sell it and keep the money from the sale of that property. You will need to obtain permission from the court for the sale, and then you must account for how the money received is being used. To get permission, you will need to ask the trustee. The trustee may decide the business property should be sold by the trustee through the bankruptcy plan instead.

- You may not incur more debt throughout the bankruptcy period. This means you cannot use your credit cards or borrow more money during the plan's lifespan unless you get the specific permission of the court and the trustee. To do that, you will need to ask the trustee in a letter and receive approval to do so from the trustee. In some cases, the courts will allow you to take on new debt; however, you need to get permission first for this, and you must provide all of the details to the bankruptcy court.

- Unexpected expenses and drops in income are also factors that need to be dealt with through the bankruptcy court when they occur during the repayment plan. This is particularly important to most small-business owners because their income fluctuates regularly. You are still expected to make your monthly payment toward your bankruptcy repayment no matter what. If you fall behind, you may need to make increased payments to catch up on the funds within a short amount of time.

If you become unable to repay your bankruptcy payment each month, you could be dropped from the Chapter 13 plan. That would make you liable for the debts you incurred, and it may signal a need to file for Chapter 7 bankruptcy. The bankruptcy court may make arrangements for a late payment, but if you are struggling to make these payments, you may need to file Chapter 7 instead.

Once you have worked through this plan, you will receive an official discharge from the bankruptcy court. The discharge releases you from obligations for any of your debt that you did not have to repay as part of the plan. It also settles and closes all debts that were satisfied. In short, this documentation will come after you have completed your three to five years of repayment. Once it arrives, the bankruptcy period officially ends.

However, this does not mean that the effects of the bankruptcy will end, nor will the overwhelming new way that you need to manage your business. The next chapter will discuss some of the problems that occur after bankruptcies are filed and how to begin to rebuild your credit.

CASE STUDY: CONSULT COUNCIL AS SOON AS POSSIBLE

Lynn A. Lape
Solo practitioner
Law Office of Lynn A. Lape
Cincinnati, Ohio
www.lynnlape.com

Lynn A. Lape, a practicing attorney who has filed bankruptcies since 1997, provides further information and insight into the bankruptcy process:

My first clients — the day after being sworn in — were bankruptcy clients. I liked them, and I sympathized with their situation, having had some hard financial times myself, because most people seemed to have something tragic happen in their lives that precipitated the financial crisis. Bankruptcy is also more black and white, in numbers, than most areas of law. I can more clearly advise people on what they can expect.

If you are thinking about filing for bankruptcy, meet with a counsel sooner than later. There are things you can do that are perfectly reasonable when you are not facing bankruptcy. But add bankruptcy to the equation, and suddenly you have a possible fraud situation. Credit counseling is now mandatory prior to filing, so look up an agency approved by the United States Trustee (UST) Program and explore that option first.

An attorney should always be used in a bankruptcy case. Too many little pitfalls can get your case dismissed without notice or a hearing. And then there are the big mistakes — from not getting the credit counseling and financial management certificates completed and filed, to not mailing the pay stubs and tax return to the trustee prior to the 341 meeting, to transferring property out of your name into someone else's, to paying back family or friends within one year prior to filing.

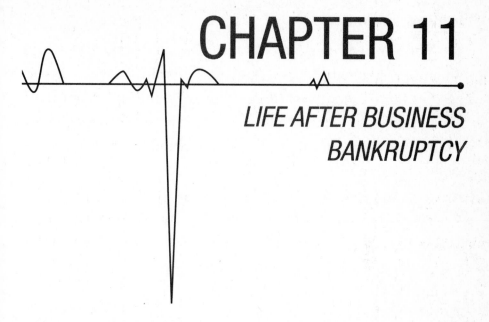

CHAPTER 11

LIFE AFTER BUSINESS BANKRUPTCY

Filing for bankruptcy can be one of the most complex aspects of your business life. You did not want this to happen to your business, but now that it has, you will need to work through the next few months and years to reestablish your business and grow your credit. As mentioned previously, bankruptcy is not the end of the line. It is a fresh start to help you to move forward.

Handling Bankruptcy-related Occurrences

There are some situations in which you could have to answer to the bankruptcy court even after you have filed bankruptcy and it has been discharged. Post-filing problems can occur without any planning or expectation from you. However, you do need to learn more about how to handle these situations.

Inherited money

It is possible for a person to inherit money or come into a large amount of money right after filing for bankruptcy. When this occurs within six months of filing Chapter 7 bankruptcy, the bankruptcy trustee may take that inheritance and use it to repay your creditors. This is shocking and can be incredibly difficult, especially if the inheritance comes from a close loved one. However, the rules of exemptions in your state still apply to these inheritances. If you have existing exemptions you have not used in total (such as not using the full exemption for tools of trade) that will protect some or all of your inheritance, you can use those exemptions to protect your inheritance.

In cases of Chapter 13 bankruptcy, the inheritance can be problematic. The first problem is that creditors may need to receive more money because they need to receive at least what they would have received through Chapter 7 bankruptcy, and your inheritance adds more value to your estate. Your disposable income has also increased. In most situations, any inheritance then needs to be paid to your creditors during a proposed plan.

Gifts

Gifts you receive after filing bankruptcy are mostly protected during the bankruptcy. Unlike inheritances, gifts are usually much lower in value. Unless the gift is quite valuable, there is likely no recourse for accepting it. This proposes a unique situation, then. If a family member would like to gift you a car or would like to give you something other of significant value, he or she can do so. There needs to be evidence, though, that another person purchased the item, such as a receipt. In some cases, if you are to lose property during a bankruptcy, your family or friends could purchase that property from the bankruptcy trustee directly and then gift the property back to you. This works well in the small business situation when you need those business assets to keep your business running.

Keep in mind that gifting your possessions to family members before bankruptcy is not advisable. The trustee may see this as an attempt to hide assets from creditors.

Increasing income

As a small business owner who has filed Chapter 7, the good news is that an increase in your income after filing and receiving a discharge of your debt does not matter at all. There is no way for creditors to claim these funds.

This is not the same for those who are filing Chapter 11 or Chapter 13 bankruptcy, though. In these situations, your disposable income is one of the key factors that affects the amount you pay your lenders each month to settle what you owe. If your income rises, the court may decide you should increase the amount of money you are paying each month. However, there are some reasons this may not happen. First, you will need to have the courts reexamine your disposable income. In most cases, this is not a problem because as your income increases, most will experience an increase in their expenses, which therefore reduces the amount of disposable income left to pay clients. For example, assume you are required to pay $500 a month toward your repayment plan based on your income and expenses. Your business begins to do well and your income rises by 10 percent. That may mean that your monthly payment of $500 needs to increase by 10 percent.

However, if your expenses have increased as well by at least 10 percent, then there is no change to the amount you need to pay to your creditors.

If there is a considerable amount of money that is coming in from your business, then the Chapter 13 bankruptcy trustee may require you to pay more toward your creditors each month.

Creditors or third parties challenging your bankruptcy

Bankruptcy comes with the benefit of protection against creditors, which comes directly from the bankruptcy filing. During the process, there is an opportunity for creditors to come to the court to file a petition or challenge the case. It is during this time that the creditor has its ability to make opinions heard.

If a creditor or a third-party collector tries to collect from you on a debt that was included in the bankruptcy after the discharge, you can prove that the creditor had his or her say by providing documentation of the bankruptcy discharge. If there are further problems, your attorney can become involved. If the creditor tries to open a hearing and it is proven that the creditor's debt was included in the bankruptcy, the bankruptcy court may instruct the creditor to pay your attorney fees for the additional work.

It is rare that any third party will come forward. Most understand the process and know that once the bankruptcy is in place, debts prior to the filing are no longer viable. Bring any circumstances like this that are repeatedly brought to your attention by the creditor to the attention of your attorney.

Getting Your Business Back On Track

Whether you have a business to run at this point is dependent on a number of factors, starting with the type of bankruptcy you filed. If you filed Chapter 7 bankruptcy, you may have liquidated all of your assets and may not have anything left to build up. In this case, opening a new business is the only option for you. Do that carefully, considering you may have limited access to funds and the fact that your previous business failed. Before planning to open a new business, keep in mind that you need to correct any problems that lead to having to file for bankruptcy in the first place.

For those in Chapter 11 or Chapter 13 bankruptcy, you do have your assets, and you can usually continue to run your business as you would under the debtor in possession contract until after your bankruptcy discharge. At that time, you regain ownership of your business from the bankruptcy estate and can maintain it as you have been. However, if your bankruptcy did affect your business, such as losing some assets or even creating a situation in which you no longer have a business, you may still have some key valuable commodities and assets that are generally not part of the business. These items need to be taken into consideration even after a Chapter 7 bankruptcy.

Business name: Although it may have very little value to anyone else, your business name has a great deal of value to you because it is how customers know you. If the business was incorporated, the corporate name is held with the state's secretary of state. That means that your business name is protected. If you filed Chapter 7, you can legally dissolve the old corporation, which will free up the business name. Then, you can incorporate a new business with the same name.

Business phone number: Even something like your business phone number is critically valuable to your business. It is your communication tool to your business's clients, after all. From the trustee's point of view, there is no value to that phone number, and the trustee may not take it from you — though it could and then make you buy it back as part of the repayment plan. If you have a dissolved business but want to start a new one using the same number, do not cut off service, nor stop paying the bill. If you stop paying the bill, you lose access to this service. Ensure that all records with the phone company put the phone number in the new business's name.

Business Web site: The same is true for a business Web site. Though it is valuable to you, it is not valuable to the trustee or anyone else, in most cases. However, if your Web site is the storefront where you sell products or it has significant income generation, it may be included in the bankruptcy. In most cases, it is not. You will need to transfer legal ownership of the Web site to your new business in the same way you would a phone number if you plan to reopen the business at some point. Otherwise, there is no benefit to keeping the Web site operational.

Business location: A business location is key to having success within your business, especially if the location is where customers meet to purchase from you. However, if you have a corporation, and the corporation owns the property, it can be difficult for you to keep the same location if the corporation is dissolved. The space itself is usually a liability to the bankruptcy trustee, though, and when the property has a very narrow resale value, the trustee will give up the rights to the property so you can use it. If you have a landlord, on the other hand, this is more complex, especially if you have stopped paying him or her. You will need to negotiate a new contract for the location after the bankruptcy discharge if your landlord is willing.

The management of your business after bankruptcy does not have to be complex. If you are unsure of your ownership in the business, the bankruptcy trustee can provide you with specific information about which assets you still own, as can your attorney.

Rebuilding Your Business Credit

In the United States, credit is at the cornerstone of a successful business. For most businesses that have gone through bankruptcy, there is no doubt that taking on new loans to reestablish themselves is a daunting task. Will you find yourself in the same position in a few years? Are lenders willing to work with you?

Before jumping into new loans, it is important to look back over the mistakes you have made and to determine how you can avoid them. This means creating circumstances for your business going forward that protect you from the mistakes that can occur in the future. Explore the following:

- What factors led to your financial problems?

- What agreements did you make with lenders that placed you in this particular position?

- Did you try to expand your business too fast?

- Did you hire too many people?

- Did you fail to keep accurate and ongoing accounting books to ensure you knew where money was flowing?

Once you understand what you did wrong, you can make plans to avoid these problems in the future. Hire an accountant if you do not have one. Learn to create reports that detail profit and labor costs, as well as maintaining inventory. If you made bad financial mistakes, such as borrowing too much money, ensure that you take steps to avoid this. Every situation is different, but focus on how you can avoid creating the same problem again.

You can do this by putting a budget in place for your business from the start. Invest in software to keep your income and expenses organized. You may need to justify hiring new employees only when the necessary funds are readily available to pay them. Minimize borrowing to start and fund your business. Make a commitment to avoid business agreements that do not offer a sizable profit margin. There is not a specific set of rules to follow to rebuild your credit after bankruptcy, but these smaller decisions will affect the whole.

Do I need credit?

Some business owners feel they do not need credit after filing for bankruptcy. They do not want to touch it for fear of what it may cause: yet another round of financial problems. However, this simply does not need to be the case. In fact, most small-business owners need to rely on credit at least somewhat to secure their businesses. Before you write off the use of credit, consider what it can do for you:

- You may need it to purchase a car.

- You may need to buy expensive equipment to keep your business operational.

- There may be a time when you want to purchase a piece of real estate for your business.

- You may need to use a line of credit with your vendors.

Most people will need credit at some point, which means you do need to work to build up your credit rating after you file for bankruptcy. There is no specific amount of gain or loss associated with bankruptcy, because credit scores are dependent on overall history, and each person will be different. It is likely, though, that your credit score will plummet deeply, sometimes by hundreds of points, after this because it shows that you made poor financial mistakes. However, it does not mean that it will stay that low. Most people will begin to see their credit scores rebound by small margins up to several hundred points within a few months to two years after filing for bankruptcy.

This is especially true if you begin to use credit. Although it may seem counterproductive to start obtaining loans again just after filing for bankruptcy, making some small, smart decisions can help you to rebuild your credit score slowly. You should not try to borrow during bankruptcy, but after bankruptcy, it is almost always necessary in order to help you rebuild your credit. You may want to open a small credit limit card and use it for minimal purchases. Pay it off in total each month. Use secured credit cards, which are backed by a deposit you make to establish the credit limit, instead of unsecured credit cards until lenders are willing to offer lower interest rates to you.

There is no law that says you are entitled to receive credit offers or credit in general after you file for bankruptcy. In fact, it is up to each lender to determine if they wish to extend a line of credit to you. Some lenders are far more liberal than others are in terms of whom they will offer credit. Some will offer credit to those who have filed for bankruptcy just six months after the business has done so. Others will not lend to anyone with bankruptcy on their credit report. However, there are thousands of lenders out there for you to try and work with. Keep in mind that time is on your side; the longer the time between the present and when you filed bankruptcy, the better.

There are several things you can do to help maximize your chances of improving your credit score. Even starting the day after you file for bankruptcy, here are some things to put into action:

- Continue to repay any and all credit lines you currently have. This includes mortgages, credit cards you reaffirmed through the bankruptcy, or other debts you still may have.

- Do not make payments late. This is one of the worst things you can do when trying to build your credit score, because it has the biggest effect on your credit score.

- When credit offers begin to arrive in the mail, consider them carefully. Do you need them? What you are likely to notice is that some credit cards that do arrive will be secured cards, which are credit cards you must put a deposit on first. The amount of the deposit is the credit line you obtain. Others will have high fees and interest rates. Picking and using one of these and making payments on time will help you to rebuild your credit, but it can be costly. Only open the lines of credit you need, which should be just one or two to start with.

- Minimize the use of your credit. Avoid maxing out credit lines. Pay off your credit lines in full every month.

- Avoid requesting numerous loans. If you need to get a new loan, do so without requesting several lines of credit at one time. This makes you seem desperate. Credit bureaus keep track of how many lenders pull reports you initiate and may downgrade your credit score if there are many.

Also important after filing for bankruptcy is to ensure you know your credit report. Each year, you are entitled legally to one credit report free from each of the three credit bureaus: Experian, Equifax, and TransUnion. Every four months, request a copy of your credit report from one of the bureaus, rotating them throughout the year. Check these credit reports for:

- **Accuracy**: Are the accounts yours and are they being reported accurately?

- **Bankruptcy discharge**: Your bankruptcy will remain on your credit report for up to ten years. During the first seven years, any debts you included in that bankruptcy filing will be reported as discharged. These debts will fall off your report after seven years.

- **Inquiries**: Ensure that the inquiries listed on your credit report are actual inquiries you requested. When you apply for any credit, a notation called an inquiry is added to your credit report. This alerts other potential lenders to your activity in applying for credit report. Only companies you specifically apply to should be listed here.

If you find errors in your credit report, contact the credit reporting agency and request that it remove them. To get a free copy of your credit report, the only Web site authorized to do so through the three major consumer credit rating companies — Equifax®, Experian®, and TransUnion® — is AnnualCreditReport (**www. annualcreditreport.com**). Any other Web site that may offer this might also be trying to sell you other services. You can find out more about credit scores and credit reports by visiting the Federal Trade Commission Web site (**www.ftc.gov**).

It takes time, but you can rebuild your credit score and improve your financial future; bankruptcy was meant to provide you with the means to do just that.

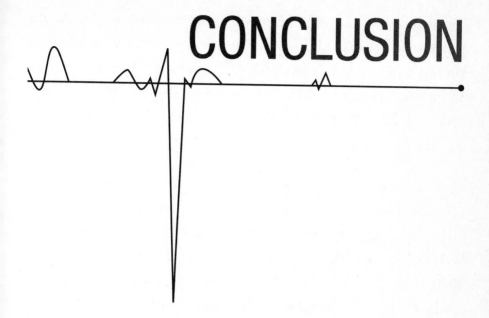

CONCLUSION

Bankruptcy seems like a finale, but it does not have to be. It is the start of your financial future, and it is an opportunity for individuals and small business owners to have a fresh start. Although bankruptcy is a serious matter and something you should not take lightly, it can be a significant opportunity for you to refresh your financial future or even breathe new life into your business.

This is not a decision you need to make too quickly or irrationally. Think about your options, consider your future, and look at your current lifestyle. Will staying on the road you are on right now with your debt continue in the long term? If you are unlikely to repay that debt and to find yourself in a better place in three to ten years, bankruptcy can help you.

The bankruptcy system in the United States is designed to provide as much protection for the creditor as is possible while still providing you with your right to have debts discharged, if in fact those debts are too great for you to be able to control. You should never rely on the bankruptcy system to solve all of your financial problems. In fact, those that file for bankruptcy too often, or try to file for bankruptcy too often, will find that this is considered abuse of the system. That could mean fraud charges, or it could simply mean the court throwing out your case.

The bankruptcy system is not simplistic in any way. There are complex elements to any type of bankruptcy you choose to file, from rules on keeping assets to managing stockholders. This is why it is incredibly beneficial for people or businesses filing for bankruptcy to hire an attorney to work for them. Your attorney will walk you through the steps of filing for bankruptcy in an initial consultation. He or she will give you the facts about whether this is a feasible option. A lawyer will provide you with the tools and information you need to make your own decision, and then he or she will work with you on the bankruptcy process, doing everything from filing your bankruptcy paperwork to representing you in court and even managing your creditors throughout the process.

You failed in your financial management, but you did not fail alone. In most areas, thousands of people file for bankruptcy each year. It is likely that at some point in most small business's lives, the business will struggle. For many small businesses and people, the need to file for bankruptcy is not something they planned for, nor could avoid. In many cases, the factors that led to filing for bankruptcy could not be controlled. Things like medical bills and a failing economic situation cause financial difficulties across the board.

Step back and consider your options. If bankruptcy is something for you, take the time right now to determine your next step. Contact an attorney; talk to your spouse; consider your business partners. Taking a step toward bankruptcy may actually mean that you are taking a step toward financial freedom.

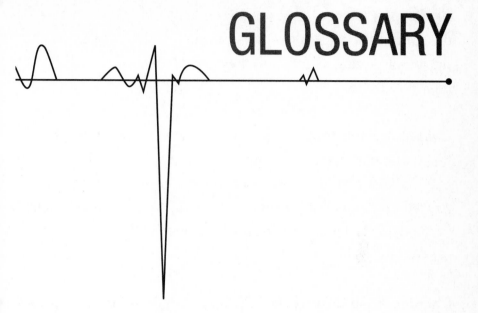

GLOSSARY

Adjustable rate mortgage: A loan where the interest rate may fluctuate throughout the lifetime of the mortgage. Often called an ARM, this type of interest rate is tied to a national index, which will cause it to increase or decrease over the lifetime of the loan. Bankruptcy cannot change this movement.

Automatic stay: A legal procedure that stops all legal proceedings against a bankruptcy filer once bankruptcy documents have been submitted to the court.

Bankruptcy estate: All property and assets included in the bankruptcy process. The person or business filing the bankruptcy will have assets placed into the bankruptcy estate until the bankruptcy trustee determines if the assets should be liquidated or maintained by the filer.

Bankruptcy trustee: A person appointed to a bankruptcy case by the courts. The trustee oversees the bankruptcy process and has the job of getting as much money as possible from the estate to repay creditors.

Chapter 7 bankruptcy: One element of bankruptcy law. Under this particular type of bankruptcy, a corporation or an individual may request that the court discharge his or her debts, especially unsecured debts. This releases the debtor from any requirement to repay these debts in the future. If available, the debtor's assets are sold to repay the debt.

Chapter 11 bankruptcy: Designed for corporations; it allows the business to reorganize debt to make it easier for repayment. This method involves more scrutiny than other forms of bankruptcy.

Chapter 12 bankruptcy: The type of bankruptcy that a farm family or business may file.

Chapter 13 bankruptcy: Allows for individuals and some small businesses to reorganize debt to make it easier to repay. Repayment of debts is necessary, in whole or in part, depending on the type of credit. It is repaid over a period of three to five years.

Collateral: Assets or property promised to a lender by a borrower as security against a loan.

Corporate shield: When a business incorporates, it provides liability protection to the business owner and shareholders within the company.

Corporation: This type of business has been given a special legal status. Corporations are businesses treated as a separate person from the business owner.

Creditor: The person or organization from whom money is borrowed.

Credit rating: A numerological formula designed to provide information on the amount of risk a person or a business is to a potential lender.

Credit report: Formulated and maintained by a credit bureau; it lists the debts and repayment history of a debtor.

Debtor: A person or a business that owes money to a creditor.

Default: When a debt is not repaid in the manner that it was agreed to at the time of securing the debt, the debtor defaults on the loan, meaning he or she does not repay the debt as required.

Discharge: During some forms of bankruptcy, debt may be discharged, or forgiven, to give the debtor a fresh start. Discharged debt does not need to be repaid.

Equity: The value of a property or asset after any loan or lien's value has been deducted.

Exemption: Property that is owned by a debtor that is protected through the filing by the bankruptcy code. Exempt property is legally allowed to be kept by the debtor after bankruptcy.

Foreclosure: A legal process that allows the lender to repossess property and land. When a mortgage debtor fails to make payment on his or her loan, the lender may initiate the foreclosure process.

Judgment: Any order by the courts that is made by the judge.

Judgment lien: A lien placed on the property that must be repaid in full prior to the sale of the property. In some cases, judgment liens can be removed during the bankruptcy process.

Lessor: A business or a person that allows someone to use property. A lessor is the property owner or manager. An exchange of use of the property for periodic payments is agreed upon. An apartment or commercial location may be leased to a person or a business by the lessor in exchange for monthly payments. In some forms of bankruptcy, leases may be broken.

Lien: A legal claim made by a creditor on the property or other assets of a person or business as a way to ensure that a debt owed is repaid. Liens may be added to a property by a creditor after filing legal action to do so. Liens may be placed on real estate, vehicles, or other assets for nonpayment of secured debts, unsecured debts, or unpaid taxes.

Meeting of creditors: Also called the Section 341 meeting; a bankruptcy hearing in which all of the filer's creditors are able to meet with the debtor and the trustee in person. The creditors are able to ask questions about the bankruptcy and about the debtor's financial affairs.

Mortgage: A loan or lien on a piece of real estate given to the creditor.

Partnership: When two or more people come together to run a business, a partnership is formed. It may be created through a legal contract or an informal agreement. Partners are personally liable for all debts within the business.

Petitioner: A request for the bankruptcy court to reduce or discharge debt for the debtor through the bankruptcy process.

Reaffirmation: An agreement that is signed during the bankruptcy process that allows for a business or an individual to reaffirm his or her commitment to repaying a loan. Debts that are reaffirmed will continue to be paid, as originally agreed, after the bankruptcy. The creditor agrees to allow the debtor to repay the loan.

Secured debt: Any type of debt backed by collateral. Property or assets are used to ensure that a debt is repaid. With secured debts, if the debtor fails to repay the debt, the creditor may repossess the property or assets to settle the debt. Common types of secured debts include mortgages, vehicles, or accounts receivable.

Sole proprietorship: A business that is owned and operated by one person. This type of business has no special legal standing. The business owner is financially responsible for the debts of the business. When filing for bankruptcy, a sole proprietor's property and assets are not protected from business creditors.

Statement of intentions: A statement or declaration made by a debtor stating how secured and other types of debts will be repaid or treated during a bankruptcy filing.

Stockholder: Anyone who owns an interest in a corporation

Tax lien: A lien placed on property or assets by a government authority because of nonpayment of taxes.

Trustee: A person or entity who has the right to property on behalf of another person or entity. A trustee in bankruptcy is a court-appointed person who will manage the bankruptcy estate of a business or person who has filed for bankruptcy. The trustee has the right to the filer's property on behalf of the creditors.

Unsecured debt: This type of debt has no security for the creditor. If the borrower defaults on repayment of the debt, the creditor has no recourse in collecting the debt against any particular asset. Unsecured debt includes credit cards, personal loans, and any other borrowed funds not secured by property.

Wage earner plan: A common name for Chapter 13 bankruptcy because the person or business filing the bankruptcy is making enough money to repay some or all of his or her debt but needs aid in repaying the debts is a different way.

Wage garnishment: A creditor's right to take all or part of a person's earnings through payroll deductions. A creditor needs to file a lawsuit against the non-paying debtor in which the creditor asks that the court require payroll deductions. If a garnishment is approved by a court judgment, the employer must take wages earned by the employee and pay them directly to the creditor. This process is used for nongovernmental organizations.

Wild card exemption: Sometimes simply called a wild card, it is an exemption used to protect a person's property or assets up to a certain value. Creditors are unable to claim property or assets of the borrower up to certain dollar amount set by the state's bankruptcy courts.

Workout program: If a debtor wishes to repay a debt after that debt has gone into default standing, he or she will work with the creditor to establish a workout program to get back on track.

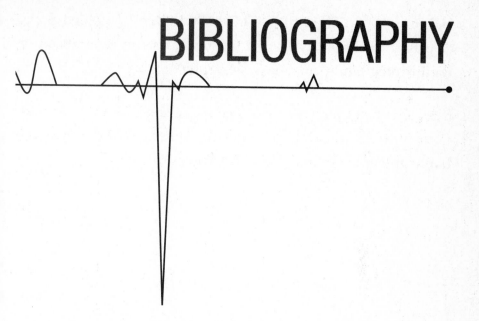

BIBLIOGRAPHY

Elias, Stephen et al. *How to File for Chapter 7 Bankruptcy*. Berkeley, California: NOLO, 2009.

Elias, Stephen and Robin Leonard. *Chapter 13 Bankruptcy*. Berkeley, California: NOLO, 2008.

Schollander, Wendell. *Bankruptcy for Small Business*. Naperville, Illinois: Sphinx Publishing, 2008.

Sommer, Henry J. *Consumer Bankruptcy*. New York, New York: John Wiley & Sons, 1994.

U.S. Courts Administrative Office. "Bankruptcy." United States Courts. 10 February, 2010. **<www.uscourts.gov/FederalCourts/Bankruptcy.aspx>**.

U.S. Courts Administrative Office. "Chapter 7." United States Courts. 10 February, 2010. <**www.uscourts.gov/FederalCourts/ Bankruptcy/BankruptcyBasics/Chapter7.aspx**>.

U.S. Courts Administrative Office. "Chapter 13." United States Courts. 10 February, 2010. <**www.uscourts.gov/FederalCourts/ Bankruptcy/BankruptcyBasics/Chapter13.aspx**>.

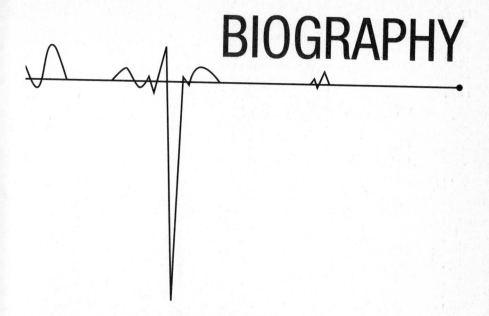

BIOGRAPHY

Sandy Baker is a freelance author specializing in consumer-related financial topics. She has ten years of freelance writing experience. Her other published titles include *The Complete Guide to Planning Your Estate: A Step-by-Step Plan to Protect Your Assets, Limit Your Taxes, and Ensure Your Wishes are Fulfilled*; *Your Complete Guide to Early Retirement: A Step-by-Step Plan for Making It Happen*; and *The Complete Guide to Wills: What You Need to Know Explained Simply*.

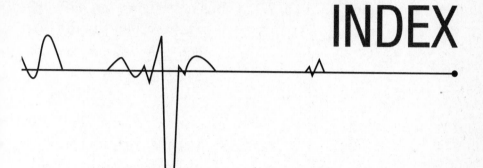

INDEX

T

U

W

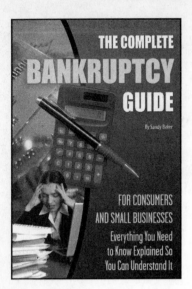

THE COMPLETE
BANKRUPTCY
GUIDE

By Sandy Baker

FOR CONSUMERS
AND SMALL BUSINESSES
Everything You Need
to Know Explained So
You Can Understand It

DID YOU BORROW THIS COPY?

Have you been borrowing a copy of *The Complete Bankruptcy Guide For Consumers And Small Businesses* from a friend, colleague, or library? Wouldn't you like your own copy for quick and easy reference? To order, photocopy the form below and send to:

Atlantic Publishing Company
1405 SW 6th Avenue
Ocala, Florida 34471-0640